CW00746476

The Godde

Nigel Pennick and Helen Field

The Goddess Year

Cover design by Daryth Bastin
Cover illustration by Nigel Pennick

Published by:

Capall Bann Publishing
Freshfields
Chieveley
Berks
RG20 8TF

Tel/Fax 01635 46455

Sol, Northern Tradition Goddess of the sun

Also by Nigel Pennick, published by Capall Bann:

Inner Mysteries of the Goths
Oracle of Geomancy
Earth Harmony 2nd ed.
Lost Lands & Sunken Cities 2nd ed.
Runic Astrology
Secret Signs, Symbols & Sigils
The New Celtic Oracle (with Nigel Jackson)

Contents

Thanks and Credits

The author wishes to thank Rosemarie Kirschmann and Prudence Jones for many useful conversations which assisted in the compilation of the material presented here. Also Helen Field for her inspired drawings of the many aspects of female divinity.

(class)

Introduction

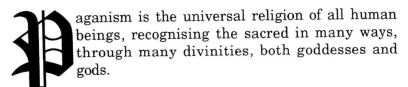aganism is the universal religion of all human beings, recognising the sacred in many ways, through many divinities, both goddesses and gods.

Paganism is the natural state of human beings, and all ancient religions, and most modern ones are Pagan, or dependent upon Pagan philosophy for their precepts.

As human beings, naturally we see the cosmos in human terms: every descriptive and belief system is essentially human in its perspectives - it cannot be otherwise.

In the traditional European view of the world, each aspect of human existence is seen symbolically reflected by a goddess or god: just as human life is equally female and male, so the world of the divine is similarly aspected.

In Nature, there are no limits: Nature is pluralistic and multivalent, an ever-changing but balanced dynamic cosmos. But in many times and places, the symbolic view of the world, which requires a certain understanding, has been overwhelmed by the literal, which requires none.

Through taking certain perceptions to be the literal, and only, truth, fundamentalism came into being - the idea that the unchangeable writings of a man-made book could be more important than the experience of human beings in Nature.

Unfortunately, this idea is at the root of most of the world's dominant religious and political systems. Also, it is basically patriarchal in nature.

Wherever such fundamentalisms exist, historically the feminine principle has been suppressed, and the worship of male-only deities enforced by men of the dominant class.

Symbolically, in the past, the various male tribal gods contended for the position in which one could become the particular god who commands and controls by drawing up end enforcing the guidelines for everything that exists. But today we live amid a plurality of 'images' from all of the known cultures of the Earth, from antiquity to the present. The days of monomania are past, and pluralism is the reality.

In the European tradition, recognition of goddesses seems to have preceded that of male gods. Many of these early 'representations' of divinity were aniconic, that is, they used something non-figurative to symbolise, rather than represent, the divine being.

For example, the image in the Cypriot temple of Aphrodite at Paphos was a meteoric stone: other deities were worshiped through sacred springs, rocks, stones and trees. Solar, lunar and stellar phenomena, too, were identified with deity, as were times of day and year.

The Anima Loci

Spirit of the wood

Later on, it became more common to personify the deities in human form, making them more accessible to people in their search for a knowledge that lies outside the individual. Today, aniconic recognition of the divine co-exists with the iconic.

Images of the Goddess such as those depicted here by the present artists serve a number of functions: they are objects of devotion, that provide psychological reinforcement for followers of the Goddess. They are also didactic expressions of the collective attributes of a certain aspect of reality, personified as the appropriate goddess.

These attributes are depicted iconically as specific objects and artifacts, or symbolically in analogous forms, colours and characters. They are not direct representations of existing physical objects: their function is to provide for a discovery of the new within the already-existent.

But it should always be borne in mind that sacred images are only part of the ceremonial environment which must attend all sacred places that acknowledge the *Anima Loci* present there, and the time, both of the day or night, and the time of year.

Images should be seen and used in the context of a complete aesthetic environment that involves all of the senses. Light, colour, texture, body movements, music, speech, incense and perfume are necessary aspects of the sacred. Awareness of time, too, is essential. This work presents both sacred images and aspects of time, both in acknowledgement of the sacred feminine in this world.

Nigel Pennick *Bar Hill, Samhain 1995 ce.*

The Circle of Space, the Eight Winds and the Welsh Tides of the day

Part One

Chapter 1

The Pagan World-View

The Pagan view of the world is that it is ensouled. It is an ancient view that all things are in some way alive. This is not to mean that literally every stone or every stream has a personality and conscious-ness like a human being: clearly, this is not so.

However, because we are living, conscious, beings, we can relate to every stone and stream in such a way. The world is not inanimate, for it relates to us through its own means. Thus, without descending into fantasy or madness, we can take the symbolic view that the earth is living, and relate to it accordingly. Thus, as an entity, the earth is personified as an anthropomorphic goddess to whom we, as humans, can relate in a creative and nurturing manner.

The materialistic view of the world, which is also a symbolic understanding, tends to lead, on the contrary,

The Runic cycle of the Moon

down the road towards destruction. When we have no personal relationship with things outside ourselves, then it is easier to treat them with disdain. We can more readily obliterate something with which we have no direct relationship.

Thus it is with the disensouled, desacralized world. Once the spirit is removed from anything, then it becomes an easy target. Tyrants know this well, for by depersonalizing their victims from names to numbers, they can more easily persuade their minions to do them to death because now they are no longer considered to be human, having been degraded into dehumanised, empty shells.

So when we recognise the transhuman dimension of existence, we are also affirming our own humanity. Many contemporary Pagans revere the female powers of nature as the Goddess, a concept that views all goddesses as aspects of one. This theology, which originates with the recognition of the goddess Isis Panthea in Alexandria in Hellenic times around 300 BCE, is one of the most widespread themes of contemporary Paganism.

It is the underlying doctrine of the Fellowship of Isis, and plays an important part in certain aspects of Wicca. But we do not need to take the view that every goddess is an aspect of the one. Each goddess represents in her own right some symbolic or mythological aspect of existence to which we can relate if we so wish.

Paganism has always been pluralistic, accepting that the existence has more than one way of doing anything. Just as there is not just a single kind of tree, herb or animal, or just one mineral on Earth, so there is not just one manifestation of divine nature.

Unlike some important contemporary religions, Paganism can never be a closed, finished system. The so-called *'religions of the book'* (different books!) that include the Jews, Muslims, Christians and Sikhs are finished systems that rely upon fixed scriptures that were assembled, edited and declared finished once and for all at a certain historical moment in time.

Subsequent to this moment, all changes in the world must be ignored by these religions, for the holy books are viewed quite literally as the last word, beyond which there can be nothing. Because of this, there can be no accommodation to new ideas and new manifestations of spirit, however transformative they may be.

The only recourse to such change that such terminally fixed religions can offer is in terms of periodic *'revivals'* or outbreaks of fundamentalism, in which the (mythological) purity of ancient times is re-imposed. Often, such revivals are conducted with a force and violence that is counter to the teachings of the religion that they seek to promote.

The other inevitable consequence of *'fixed book'* religion is that over time they fragment into increasing numbers of sects, each of which claims to have exclusive access to the true interpretation of scriptures that, with the passing of time, become more remote from the individual's experience of everyday life.

To Pagans, however, it is a quite simple procedure to accept deities from new or exotic systems, and to adapt with regard to human progress wherever it may occur.

This is how Roman Paganism operated, where goddesses and gods of other peoples, such as the Celts, were fitted in

·UNICORN AND MY LADY· BY MARY FIELD·

Unicorn and My Lady

Fjorgynn the Earth Mother

The Goddess as Fountain of Wisdom

to the Pantheon, either in terms of Roman deities - the *Interpretatio Romana* - or as divinities in their own right.

The Brazilian Candomble religion, too has assimilated Christian saints and deities into the Pagan framework of this strong pluralism, where everything is what it is, and accepted as such by all in society, is the only way that belief can exist within contemporary society, in peaceful co-existence.

If pluralism is not accepted by all members of society, then society itself ceases to exist. Instead, the country disintegrates into a power struggle between opposing factions of its inhabitants, leading, ultimately to the unsavoury result of *'ethnic cleansing'*.

This occurs when any group sets up its own belief as possessing the absolute, unchanging, non-negotiable, truth, which must be imposed on non-believers as a matter of religious duty. Unlike the *'one-way'* religions, Pagan pantheons are quite capable of absorbing other divinities, viewing them as alternative mythologies that contain some essence of whatever archetype they represent. The traditional year relates spiritual qualities to their corresponding times, and each of these times is commemorated by a festival or observance.

Each festivity is ruled over by an appropriate, corresponding god and goddess. This book is primarily about these goddesses, within the European tradition, which has continued for at least 100,000 years, and lives today.

Diana, the huntress

Lady Bountiful

Epona

Rhiannon

The Fox Goddess

The Swan Maiden

Sirona, goddess of holy wells

THE WHEEL, AND "URD, VERDANDI, + SKULD."

The Norns' Wheel

The Mermaid

Walpurgisnacht

Chapter 2

The Goddess Time-Cycle

lthough its precise antiquity is uncertain, the eightfold year is an integral part of contemporary European Paganism. This eightfold year is composed of four solar festivals, or 'quarter days', marking the crossing-and turning-points of the sun in the annual cycle, and four 'fire' festivals, otherwise called 'cross-quarter days'.

The four 'quarter days' are determined by the dynamic movement of the Earth around the Sun. They are the solstices, the longest and shortest days, and the two equinoxes, transition-points that mark half-way between the solstices.

The year's light is divided into the shorter and longer halves by the equinoxes, which are the only two days in the year when there is 12 hours daylight and 12 hours darkness. The spring equinox marks the time of year when the light is growing longer; before it, nights are longer than days; after it, days are longer than nights.

Isis

The Northern Tradition Runic Wheel of Time and Space

Sekhmet

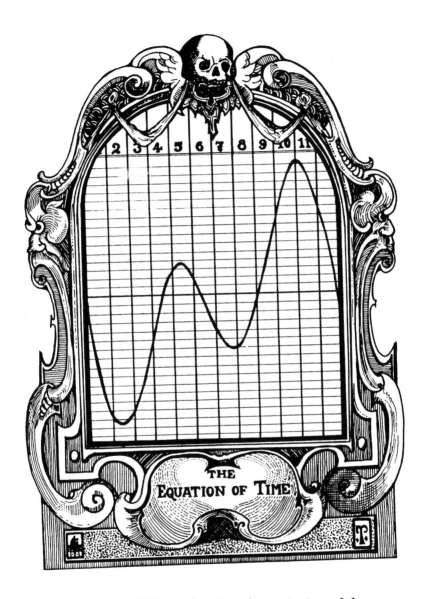

The Equation of Time, showing the variation of the mean clock time from the true solar time during the yearly cycle

Bastet, goddess of cats

The half of the year that the spring equinox divides is the period when the light is increasing after the shortest day of the winter solstice.

The summer solstice is the apex of the light, the longest day at which the declining half of the year begins. The days get shorter now, and at the autumnal equinox, the dark half of the year, where days are shorter than nights, is entered.

Day length declines and night length increases until the winter solstice, which is the shortest day, bracketed between the longest nights. After this, day length increases again, with a corresponding decline in night length.

Thus the year can be seen as divided into two different halves by the four 'quarter days'. The half of increase runs from the winter solstice until the summer solstice, whilst the half of decrease runs from the summer solstice to the winter. The year also consists of a dark and light half.

Between the autumnal equinox and the vernal (spring) equinox is the dark half of the year, when the days are shorter than the nights. The light half of the year begins at the vernal equinox, and runs until the autumnal one. This is the period when daylight is longer than the nights. In religious terms, the solstices, especially midwinter, are associated with male deities.

The four 'fire festivals' come between the solstices and the equinoxes. They are not so obviously related to astronomical phenomena as the solstices and equinoxes, being earthly rather than celestial festivals, related to the cycle of the harvest in central and northern Europe.

Hertha

Juno

The Labyrinth: springtime image of the Goddess

Luna, Goddess of the moon

Cybele and her dragons

Blodeuwedd

Lilith

Fairy

Also, they do not exactly halve the periods between them, rather they are observed around 40 days after the previous 'quarter day' and 50 days before the next one. This may be explained by changes in the calendar since they were instituted in antiquity.

The four 'fire festivals' have various alternative names. The first in the traditional year is at its beginning, November Eve. It is Samhain, known widely also by its old English name of Hallowe'en.

Next comes February Eve, otherwise called Imbolc, Brigantia or Candlemas. The third 'fire festival' is May Day, Beltane; whilst the last is the festival of harvest, Lammas or Lughnassadh, celebrated on August 1st.

In the Northern Tradition, festivals like these begin at sunset on the eve of the day which is their main celebration. This custom is reflected today in the vernacular use of terms such as 'Christmas Eve'.

Symbolically, the festival begins in darkness, just as the child gestates in the womb, before coming into the light when the time is right. Thus, dawn on the festival day is preceded by gestation in darkness, reflecting the natural order of things in a truly Pagan way.

Each of the 'fire festivals' occupies a place in the year where two influences, dark or light and increase or decline are present. In this way, each festival reflects the European tradition of the fourfold, working in a manner comparable with the way that the four elements influence one another to create the four humours. In contrast with the male aspect of the solar festivals, these four 'fire festivals' are ruled by goddesses.

Frigg, riding her distaff

Their annual cycle relates to the cycle of the moon, waxing and waning. Thus, according to one aspect of European Paganism, Samhain, in the dark half of the year and also the declining light, is associated with the goddess Hecate or the Cailleach, goddess of the Old Moon.

It is the festival of the dead, the time of year when the barrier between the material world of the living and the Otherworld of the shades and spirits is at its thinnest.

The next festival, Brigantia, is the feast-day of Bride or Brigid, the virgin or young woman. In lunar terms, she is the Young Moon. Brigantia is the time when the first stirrings of life are noticeable in the earth, with the lengthening of the days after dark January.

May Day sees the choosing of the May Queen, with the inherent lusty power of the Maying ceremonies. She is the Moon in her rapidly waxing state. Now is the time of joyful sexuality, brightness and hope.

The final *'fire festival'*, Lammas, is the time when the pregnant earth gives up her harvest, signifying the Moon in her waning condition.

As with all symbolic systems, the lunar or female cycle can be related to the *'cross quarter days'* of the year in other ways as well.

The rich symbolic validity of spiritual systems often allows new insights to emerge from traditional explanations. This cannot happen in spiritual systems that insist upon the primacy of texts.

The Owl Goddess, an aspect of Athena / Minerva

The labyrinth of Midsummer

Sol, Goddess of the Sun

Furrina and her otter

Cerridwen and her cauldron

The Goddess in the Labyrinth

Thus, Samhain can symbolise menstruation; Brigantia the commencement of ovulation, with the release of the virgin ovum; Beltane as the time of fertilisation, in the Maying rites.

Beltane is the point at which the male and the female cycles interact, when the Maypole is planted in the Earth. The fourth, and final, part of this cycle is at Lammas, seen as the time when the festilize ovum embeds itself in the womb.

The specific parts of the lunar cycle, and hence, by implication, the year, are ascribed to certain classical European goddesses whose attributes most closely symbolise the state of the moon at that time. The first three days of the Moon are sacred to Persephone, in her aspect as the initiatrix of things. Then days four to six come under the regency of Artemis, the goddess who empowers the newly-planted seed.

Days seven to nine are ruled by Kore, who is the Maiden of Menarche, linking the states of childhood and adulthood. Next, days ten to twelve are under the regency of Hera, who as Queen of Heaven and creatrix, expresses the awesome power of creation.

On days thirteen to fifteen, Demeter, the nurturer, rules. She is followed on lunar days sixteen to eighteen by the earth-goddess Gaia. After Gaia, the days of waning, nineteen to twenty-one, are under the rulership of the old woman Hestia, who is the grandmother who both protects and rules her children and grandchildren.

Darkening days twenty-two to twenty-four are ruled by the gorgon Medusa, crone-figure of death and the

Diana the Huntress

separation of spirit from matter. She is the destroyer, who brings cycles to an end so that new ones can commence in their place.

Lunar days twenty-five to twenty-seven are under the regency of Hecate, queen of the otherworld who rules over the shades of the departed. Finally, the remaining, dark, days of the Moon are comparable to the 'secret of the unhewn stone' in the Celtic tree calendar. They are ruled by the ineffable, unknowable goddess who is only recognisable through the mask that she wears.

Freyja, on her Siberian Tiger

The witch, embodiment of the power of the Goddess

Cerridwen, with her cauldron of inspiration

Sequana, Goddess of the River Seine

The Vampire

Howling at the Moon

Samhain Eve

The Lunantishees, guardian spirits of the blackthorn

Hela

Chapter 3

The Goddesses of Nature

In the European Pagan tradition, each deity rules over or symbolises a specific aspect of existence. These powers are celebrated in Celtic, Teutonic and Nordic writings, folk-tales and traditions. Partly because the patriarchal Christian religion was so dominant in Europe for so long, the part that the female plays in sacred life is still rather suppressed.

But since Robert Graves suggested in his seminal book on the indigenous European world-view, *The White Goddess* that perhaps it would be for the best if the religion of the goddess should be reinstated as Europe's faith, there has been a resurgence in the recognition of the feminine side of the sacred.

This re-emergence has brought into being a fresh religious interpretation that has parallels in the Americas in those religions where the West African deities of the Yoruba tradition have merged with the Catholic pantheon as *orixas*.

Irnan the Sorceress

Thus, in the candomble religion of Bahia in Brazil, the Catholic St Anna, mother of Mary, is Nanan, the oldest of the *orixas*, mother of Omolu, the *orixa* healers.

In the northern European pantheon, the Catholic St Anna is the goddess Anna, ancestress of the royal line of Celts. Thus, an adherent of Candomble can venerate Nanan at a Catholic shrine of St Anna, just as a European Pagan will revere her image as the Celtic ancestral goddess.

Thus, holy places of saints, *orixas*, ancestors, goddesses and gods are worshipful to more people than just those who belong to the religion that administers the shrine. Ultimately, because Nature is pluralistic, it is only a matter of human theological interpretation that makes people differ over the nature of gods and goddesses.

The removal of certain saints from the Catholic pantheon, like St George and St Barbara has meant that they have passed into a post-Christian condition. Yet they still exist as spiritual beings, with their devotees.

They are not Pagan deities in the strict since, but have the orlog of their Pagan and Christian past. That they function as deities or *orixas* is undisputed, and it is possible to come into a personal spiritual relationship with them as well as with any other holy being. No religion is static, and as it grows the restored European Paganism will develop into something unprecedented, yet retaining the essential traditions and meanings of the spiritual current of which it is representative.

This book is part of that recognition.

The spirit of the Labyrinth

A full exposition of the historical background of this tradition can be found in Prudence Jones and Nigel Pennick's book, *A History of Pagan Europe* (Routledge, 1995), and further elements in Nigel Pennick's *The Oracle of Geomancy, The Inner Mysteries of the Goths* and *Secret Signs, Symbols and Sigils* (all Capall Bann, 1995).

When analysed according to modern ideas of taxonomy, the deities of the Northern Tradition fall into three main categories. At the most basic are the elemental deities and powers. These also appear to be the most archaic. They include the ice, fire and earth-giants, and elemental beings that can scarcely be imagined in human form. They are so archaic that any collective name they may have had is lost.

More human in their attributes are the earth-oriented deities of the nomadic pursuits of gathering, hunting and fishing, known by their Norse name, the Vanir. In the Nordic religion, these Elemental deities and the Vanir were overtaken and absorbed by the goddesses and gods of the settled life based on agriculture.

Their Nordic name is the Aesir, the famous deities of Norse sagas and the organised Northern Heathenism of Scandinavia and England. They are often seen patriarchally, with the gods Odin and Thor as leaders. But the goddesses of the Aesir, the Asyniur, of whom Frigg is the most notable, are *"no less important than the gods"*.

The traditional European theory of the composition of existence is that it consists of a fixed number of *'elements'*, which combined in various ways, *'produce'* the multiple things of existence. Basically, this idea represents the early beginnings of a reductionism that led to modern western science. Taken literally, it leads to a barren, materialistic, view of existence, but used in context as a hypothetical model (as in the ancient mystery-traditions), it is of great value.

The classical European view is of the four elements Fire, Air, Water and Earth. In the Northern Tradition, influenced by the icy winters of northern Europe, a fifth element, Ice, is added sometimes to the other four.
Although they increase in density from fire at the lightest to earth at the heaviest, there is no 'league table' of value - each of these elements are of equal value. Similarly, the senses to which each element relates are also of equal value.

The image of the elemental goddess signifies the equal importance of all of the senses, a concept often over-ridden by the contemporary insistence on the visual. Traditionally (unlike the scientific-reductionist world view), the elements are not there to be measured for representation.

They exist, so far as defined by human consciousness, separate from the concerns and needs of humans, manifesting when and how they will.

The elements symbolise direct experience, unsullied by the filter of spectacle: the effect of certain aspects of the seamless flow of existence on the senses, without commentary or editing. At its most intense, it is the epiphany of the goddess, overwhelming presence.

Such an experience is reported by the twelfth-century Christian mystic Hildegarde von Bingen:

70

"Then I saw a most glorious light and in it a human form of sapphire hue, all aflame with a most gentle glowing fire, and the fire was infused in the glorious light: and both light and fire transfused that human form - all interexistent as one light, one virtue and one power".

In marked contrast to the direct experience of the transcendent undergone by mystics, contemporary representation through the electronic media is indirect and fragmented. In every branch of the contemporary media, the image itself is not represented directly: it is reduced to a succession of projected frames or digitized as in film, television, computer games and so-called *'virtual reality'*.

None of these representations present reality, but contain inherent within themselves the dissonant effects of discontinous flicker. They are deconstructed fragmental representations of visual images that are presented as reality. In this screen-based re-presentation, we suffer the unavoidable suppression of the senses of smell, taste, bodily feeling, sense of direction and, to some extent, hearing.

We are at some considerable distance from the seamless, direct experience that is symbolised by the Elemental Goddess.

In contemporary society, Paganism offers ways that question the illusions of representation; they need not be dislocated as are most contemporary manifestations of presentation.

As models of direct, real experience, elemental deities represent the spiritual aspects of material existence. In the Norse system, there are five deities: two are goddesses, and three are gods.

Erda is the goddess of the living, bounteous earth, and Rinda is goddess of the frozen earth. Loge is god of wild-fire, often assimilated with the trickster-god Loki. He has two daughters by Glut (*"Glow"*).

They are Eisa, goddess of the embers, and Einmyria, to whom the ashes are sacred. The deity Hlora, foster-mother of Thor, is the personification of heat.

The precise nature of these deities are part of the complex description of reality that appears symbolically throughout Northern Tradition spirituality.

Glut, burning matter, gives out light (Loge) and heat (Hlora), leaving embers (Eisa), which still give some light and heat, and finally ashes (Einmyria), which, whilst undisturbed, still contain the pattern of Glut.

This pattern, the residual information, is significant in the legend of the binding of Loki when he flees after causing the death of Balder. There appears to be no parallel of these alchemical deities in the Celtic tradition.

The Norse god Kari is deity of the air, and Hler is god of the waters, parallelling the Celtic sea-god, Lir. In contemporary Paganism, the pentagram symbolises these five primal elemental deities.

Most fundamental to us all is the female principle of the Earth. She is called many names in the European Pagan tradition, *inter alia*, Gaea, Tellus Mater, Erda, Nehalennia, Nerthus, Jorö, Fjorgynn, Will's Mother and Zemyna.

The Irish goddesses of the land, Eriu, Banba and Fodla, are local manifestations of this Earth Mother. As Hertha, she is the goddess of the hearth. Throughout the world, in places where patriarchal religion has not driven her veneration underground, her acknowledgement is paramount. But whether she is acknowledged or not, it is a fact that all life on this planet comes from the Earth Mother, and returns to her.

Tirelessly, she nourishes plant, animal and human life. Without her, there could be no existence. In the Northern Tradition, she is personified as the Goddess Jorth.

In another aspect, Fjorgynn, Mother Earth, she is mother of the goddess Frigg and Asa-Thor.

Fjorgynn is guardian of the cauldron of rebirth, and the woven basket containing the fruits of the earth. She is flanked by pottery vessels, made from the clay of Mother Earth. These are the human forms of male and female, receptacles of spirit.

In the icon reproduced here, Fjorgynn holds the youthful goddess and god. Frigg is goddess of settled life. She holds the distaff, traditional symbol of womanhood. As giver of flax to humankind, Frigg taught our ancestors to grow, harvest, process, spin and weave the material, enabling us to clothe ourselves. Her patterns adorn and inform the artifacts of women's handicrafts. In her cosmic aspect, Frigg is also Queen of Heaven, holder of silent knowledge. Her cloak is the starry heavens, her spindle the Pole Star.

The young Thor carries the hammer Mjollnir. He personifies the power of the *Hammermen*, who, through their physical strength, learning and skills (craft), alter the physical world to create objects for human use. Using the hammer, symbol of order, the craftsman brings human order from the quite different *'chaos'* of natural materials.

The hammer of Thor represents the male power, which uses physical strength and the *'hammering action'* of many male activities. This contrasts with the *'winding action'* of the traditional female crafts of sowing grain, spinning, weaving, knitting, basket-making and pottery.

It was through the female crafts that the inner wisdom-teachings of the Goddess were preserved in times when patriarchal theocratic governments attempted to suppress them.

Many of the individual goddesses of Nordic religion and later Germanic Heathenism can be seen as aspects of this goddess - Mother Earth.

Not strictly deities, but aspects of them, are the elemental giants and giantesses, such as Surt, the fire-giant and the hermaphroditic primal giant, Ymir, from whose dismembered corpse the physical earth was formed.

The primary deities of the Vanir are Freyja and Frey, whose names mean *"the Lady"* and *"the Lord"*. These are identical with the Lady and Lord of contemporary Wicca. They represent the balanced female-male aspects of the living, organic, world.

Freyja is goddess of the earth's plant-life, the trees and animals of the woodland, female sexuality, natural love, and the arts of magic. She is the patroness of *seiör*, the archaic trance-magic technique which comes from the older times, the age of the elemental deities.

Freyja is one of the ancient goddesses of northern Europe. She is a Vanic goddess stemming from pre-agricultural times, representing the qualities and values of the ancient society of hunters. She is goddess of love, free sexuality, fertility, shamanic magic and hunting. Her name means *The Lady*, corresponding with her consort-brother Frey, *The Lord*.

Freyja's attributes can be contrasted with those of the goddess Frigg, who is the goddess of agricultural civilisation, the traditional married life of the woman in a settled, state. She is depicted sometimes in a chariot or cart pulled by cats. Also she is shown riding a cat or tiger. Frig rides a distaff, symbol of the woman's craft of spinning thread.

In eastern and south-eastern Europe, the goddess riding a great cat is the Great Goddess Cybele, depicted mounted upon a lion or tiger. She was venerated in central Europe as well as the south, and one of her cultus-objects is extant as the Gundestrup Cauldron, made by co-operating Celtic and Slavic craft-workers. These connections indicate the difficulty in making hard-and-fast distinctions between the goddesses, for all can be viewed as multivalent aspects of the archetypal Goddess who manifests daily in many ways around us.

Freyja is the archetypal wise woman. She wears a talismanic necklace, Brisingamen. She flies with the use of a falcon-skin; she instructs the gods in the use of magic charms and the creation of potions; and she calls up magic fire. Her sybilline qualities, those of Cybele, are recalled in local legends in Germany and Scandinavia.

In the image here, based on the medieval wall-painting in Schleswig Cathedral, iconic conventions are followed. The goddess is shown full-faced.

She carries a horn, multivalent symbol of summoning and plenty. Although she is blowing it, it does not obscure the divine face. Her ride on the tiger incorporates the wild elements of the hunter that honours the hunted beast in mystical rapport, taking only that which is necessary to sustain life. It also recalls the cat as sacred familiar animal of the witch.

A number of goddesses and gods are sacred in the ancient European traditions of hunting. In addition to Freyja, there are the British deity, Herne the Hunter, the Gallo-Celtic deity Cernunnos and the southern European goddess Diana the Huntress. Furthermore, British Bardic tradition describes hunting as one of the three pursuits of sustenance:

> *"Three pursuits are free to a Bard, and to every other native of country and nation, namely: hunting; agriculture; and pastoral cares;*
>
> *for it is by means of these that all men obtain sustenance, and they ought not to be forbidden to any one who may wish them".*

Triads of Bardism and Usages No. 23.

Today, Freyja is the symbol of rapport with Nature, not by attempting to command and control her, but existing in an harmonious partnership, taking from Nature, but also giving to Nature. She denotes the possession of power and strength without using it to dominate, abilities harnessed to necessity, not for self-seeking, one-sided mastery over Nature and other sentient beings.

In this Age of Representation, Freyja is a reminder that modernity, in which the world is reduced to a picture, existing only through representation, creature of man's creation, is not reality, but a pale and distorted reflection of it.

According to Norse mythology, the goddess Freyja has two lovers: her twin brother, Frey, and Odur. Frey is the god of growth, male sexuality and the fruitful rain.
The goddesses Hnossi ("*Jewel*") and Gersemi, Freyja's two daughters by Odur, govern all beautiful, wonderful, things in the natural world.

Freyja rides the world in a chariot pulled by two grey wildcats, and at Schleswig, she is depicted riding on a huge striped cat like a Siberian tiger.

She also flies shape-shifted, in the form of a Peregrine Falcon. She wears the necklace Brisingamen, her magical power-object.

Flidhair, deity of forest animals, is a Celtic goddess whose attributes are similar to Freyja. Like some other Northern deities, Freyja has several by-names, among which are Friagabis, Horn, Mardel, Skjalf, Syr and Thrung. Another Vanic goddess, worshiped in Heligoland, is Thorgerda, who seems to have been associated with free sexuality.

Chapter 4

The Queen of Heaven and Other Divinities

The Aesir and Asyniur are the deities of agricultural life, trade, law and war. There are many known deities: some lesser ones are viewed as aspects of others. The chief goddess is Frigg (*"Most Magnificent"*), Queen of Heaven. She is the patroness of the growing crops, food-preparation, cloth-making and procreative sexuality.

The distaff and spindle, upon which thread is spun are her magic tools. Her cloak is the night sky, spangled with stars. She wears Heron plumes, a golden girdle and a bunch of keys. Heron plumes are a symbol of silent knowledge. They are the Norse equivalent of the Crane Bag of Secrets in the Celtic mysteries, relating her to the Goddess in the Labyrinth, the place of the crane dance. (See The New Celtic Oracle)

Frigg's palace is called Fensalir, and she is also worshiped under the name of Zisa, whose shrine in Pagan times was at Augsburg. Frigg is associated with several specialised goddesses, who are sometimes seen only as aspects of her.

Frigg's function as Queen of Heaven (ruler of time) is personified in Saga, the goddess of events in time. She is the goddess of memory, representing the store of memory in human culture, sayings, re-tellings, the oral tradition of culture often maintained in women's collective work. She is goddess of the geomythic understanding of the landscape, the hoard of incidents, legends, stories and names that make up any journey across our own land.

Frigg's aspect as bringer of information, or messenger-goddess is Gna (Divine Grace), the personification of the refreshing breeze, who rides high on the horse Hofvarpnir ("*Hoof-Thrower*"). She brings good news and help, a change for the better, "*a breath of fresh air*", replenishing us with the ond of divine providence.

The Celtic horse-goddesses Epona and Rhiannon share some of her attributes, recalling the close affinity between women and horses still present among the East Anglian horse-charming wise women until the present day. Fulla, otherwise known as Volla or Abundantia attends Frig as her jewel-casket-bearer.

This golden-haired deity is symbolic of the fullness of the earth provided for us by the goddess of fertility, who in the Classical tradition is called Demeter or Ceres. Her hair, bound by a golden circlet, represents the bound sheaf at harvest-time.

The three goddesses, Saga, Gna and Fulla, are the northern versions of the Classical '*Three Graces*'. They recall other triadic or triple goddesses like the Greek

Hecate, the Fates and the threefold Celtic goddesses like the Three Machas and the Matron's.

Other members of the Nordic Asyniur symbolise what we need to provide for human life. Hlin, whose name means Flax, (which gives us linseed, and linen for clothes, sails and rope) brings infinite compassion to those whom Frigg favours. Hlin has the power to rescue us when the situation appears hopeless. She is the goddess of rings.

The ring symbolises enclosure and protection, the power of relating to the divine force of compassion. Inside this ring, we are at another level, invulnerable to the wounds of the world.

Her mystery is that of the Arctic Circle, the ring in which darkness and night is defeated in summer time with the Midnight Sun, and so she is a midsummer goddess.

Gentle wisdom is the realm of Snotra, the goddess of the language of the birds, whose bird is the goose. Gefn ("*The Bountiful Giver*") is the goddess of gifts. Her X symbol, the rune Gyfu, is the sacred mark of Northern Tradition religion. Hers is the horn of plenty, containing the products of the Earth such as jewels and metals, and the products of the harvest. She is paralleled by the Celtic goddesses, Rosmerta, regent of material wealth, and Brigantia (Christianised as St Brigit), goddess of learning, poetry and handicrafts, the producers of wealth both on the material and intellectual planes.

Other Celtic goddesses that bring useful things and pleasure are Be Find, Clidna and Fand. The Nordic goddess Sjofn is the deity of love, for in her we see beauty as the natural result of love. Gefjon is goddess both of the plough and of unmarried women. Lofn brings together men and women in love in conditions where marriage is forbidden or impossible.

Hers is the transcendent love that crosses the boundaries of the standards of social correctness. Eir (Eyra or Airmed) is goddess of healing and medicine, gatherer of the holy herbs. *"Gaping wounds are bound by Eyra"*. It is from her that medicine was taught to women, to whom it was an exclusive art in former times. Hers is the blood-staunching stone once prized by every warrior and harvest-worker. (For more details of such blood-stones, see the author's *Secrets of East Anglian Magic*, Robert Hale, 1995).

Nordic power comes through the agency of the goddess Thrud. She is sister to Hlora (Lorride), whilst Grid, the giantess goddess who symbolises pressure is the third in this trinity. Thrud is part of the fire-working complex that includes Loge, Glut, Eisa, Einmyria, Hlora and Thor, god of the hammermen. Two sister goddesses command oath-taking and breaking.

Vor (*"Faith"*) is the divine witness to oaths, and her sister Var or Vara, the divine punisher of those who break them. Vor has the power to see through deception, whilst Var, goddess of awareness, sees things clearly, *as they are,* without prejudice. She is goddess of business institutions. Syn guards the door, admitting desirable people and things, whilst keeping out the undesirable. Like the Roman goddess Carna, she is patroness of bolts and locks, and is worshiped at the beginning of June.

As the golden-haired swan-goddess, patroness of the ripe grain, Sif rules over the bright, fertile days of summer, and the first harvest day of Lammas. She is a bringer of peace and happiness, being closely allied to Fulla. Nanna represents the fertility of earthly vegetation opposite Balder's solar power.

Sol is goddess of the sun; Bil, the daughter of the Moon. Iduna sustains the divine world through her daily gift of the golden apples of eternal life. A little-known fragment links her with the discovery of the runes. Bestla is mother of the gods Odin, Vili and Ve, the Sons of Bor.

There are numerous water-divinities in the Northern Tradition. Each represents a different aspect of water. Most archaic is the primal elemental deity, Hler, The major Aesir water-deities are Ran and Aegir. The goddess Ran, destroyer of ships, represents death for all who perish at sea. She is the goddess of gold, *"the flame of the sea"*. Her magic *'tool'* is the fishing-net, which she invented.

Ran's male counterparts are Aegir, god of the stormy sea, whose emblem is a grappling-iron, and Njord, deity of coastal waters. In the Celtic tradition, many river-goddesses are still recalled,. For instance, the great rivers of mainland Europe, the Don and Danube, are sacred to the Celtic goddess Dana, as is the River Don that flows through Doncaster in England.

In France, Axona is goddess of the Aisne and Sequana of the Seine. In Ireland, Sinend is goddess of the Shannon, whilst in Britain, the goddess Deva rules the river Dee and Belisama the Mersey.

In the Nordic interpretation of existence, the fresh waters beneath the earth, are ruled by Mimir, who although often portrayed as male, was originally seen as female. Mimir's power is at the primal depths of being, present in the önd of holy wells and mineral waters. His/her sacred objects are an axe and a crown of sea-shells.

In mainland Europe, the Celtic goddess Sirona rules over holy wells in which the power of the sun is present. Sul is the ruler of the hot springs at Bath, and in the *Interpretatio Romana*, she is assimilated with the Roman goddess Minerva. The well-goddesses are is paralleled in the south by the goddess Furrina, who is acknowledged in a festival in late July.

In the Nordic interpretation, the waves of the sea are known as *"Aegir's Daughters"*. According to Norse mythology, nine wave-maidens were the mothers of Heimdall. They are called Atla, Augeia, Augiafa, Egia, Gjalp, Greip, Jarnsaxa, Sindur and Ulfrun. Other groups of demi-goddesses are the Tree-Maidens and the Valkyries, choosers of those who die in combat.

Similarly, there are nine Disir. These goddesses, whose name means *"the Shining Ones"*, are personal *'guardian angels'* who watch over various aspects of existence and human life. They include the Horse Dis, Jodis (Holda), whose face is half black and half white like the underworld goddess Hela; Vanadis (Freyja); Olgefjon (Groa), the vegetation Dis; Ondurdis (the snow Dis); Sinmara (the night Dis); Idis (Sunna) and possibly Iduna.

In some ways, they parallel the Nine Muses of Classical Paganism. The Disir are acknowledged by their festival on February Eve, called Imbolc or Brigantia in the Celtic tradition. The giant Jokul (Glacier) has three wintry daughters, all of whom are aspects of snow and ice: Fonn, Drffa, and Mioll.

Three other sisters are the Weird Sisters or Norns, who often are thought of as principles rather than strictly anthropomorphic goddesses. But, equally, they must be considered divine. Like their southern European counterparts, the Moirae and the Fates, the Norns are the guardians of time and fate.

They are the rulers over the whole year, throughout which beginnings and endings are always taking place. Each fate or Norn signifies one of the three stages of existence, for everything must have a beginning, a middle, during which it is in continuance, and finally, an end.

The beginning Norn is Urd, 'that which was'; the present is represented by Verdandi, *'that which is becoming'*; and the future is symbolised by Skuld, *'that which is to come'.* They are the threefold aspects of woman: the grandmother (Urd), the mother (Verdandi), and the daughter (Skuld). Magically, they are represented by three cords. Urd, the origin, has a white cord; Verdandi, the sustainer, a red one, and Skuld, the maiden-destroyer, has black one.

The three Norns are sometimes seen as aspects of the primal goddess named Wyrd or Wurt, ultimately parts of the virtues of Mother Earth. The Celtic Mothers are usually depicted as three goddesses, and to this day Y Mamau is the traditional Welsh name for the fairies.

Nott is the goddess of the darkness of night, the mother of Day. Each night is sacred to her. Skadi, whose name means *'shadow'*, is the Nordic warrior-and hunting-goddess of winter-time who travels the icy wastes on her skis and skates. She is the destroyer, bringer of dark and destructive magic. Her powers and attributes parallel those of the Celtic martial artist or shield-maiden,

Scathach, who in the *Ulster Cycle* teaches the hero Cu Chullain fighting techniques on the Island of Skye.

Ruler of death and keeper of the underworld is Hela, daughter of the giantess Angurboda, whose name means *"Portender of Evil"*. She rules the shade-world of Niflheim, but as the personification of death, has power over all the Nine Worlds.

In times of famine, she rides the world on a three-legged horse, using her broom to sweep the dead into the underworld, the bridge into which is guarded by the goddess Mordgud. In Celtic tradition, she parallels the female destructive principles such as Black Annis and the Morrigan, the latter of whom, along with her two companion battle-goddesses, the Badb and Nemain, brings victory to those whom she favours, and death to those whom she deems to be the losers.

The related Nordic goddess Sigyn (*"Giver of Victory"*) is known as the faithful consort of the trickster-god Loki, like the black battle-raven so much associated with mass combat in ancient Europe. Another hag-aspect of the underworld is Elli, personification of old age, bringer of death by a means seemingly more natural than violence. Another dark Nordic figure is Thokk (*"Coal"*) is giantess of the underworld who refused to weep at the death of Balder.

The female *'choosers of the slain'* are the Valkyries. There are up to 16, though 9 is the usual number. Among them are Alvit, Bodvild, Brunhild, Hildr, Hlokk, Guth, Olrun, Svanhvit and Rota. Occasionally, Skuld, the third Norn is included with the Valkyries. Sometimes, they appear in swan-form, as do the Children of Lir in Irish myth.

The Northern Tradition recognises many other goddesses and gods that cannot be classified among the Elementals, Vanir, Aesir or Asyniur. Menja and Fenja were the giantesses who worked Frodi's mill, grinding the salt of the sea.

The Germanic goddesses Walburga, a lunar deity, and Eostre (Ostara), divinity of the dawn and springtime are remembered each year at the festivals which bear their names: Walpurgisnacht (May Eve) and Easter. Nehallennia, the Frisian goddess of the sea and vegetation, is an aspect of the Earth Mother mentioned above. Her sacred images show her accompanied by a dog and a basket of apples. Like Skadi, she is a holy island goddess.

Holda (Frau Holle or Hulda) presides over the weather, dispensing good things to human beings. She rules over the Huldrafolk (the dwarves and elves). Her attendants are crowned with the Alpine Rose, her sacred flower.

Elden (Elaine or Helen), goddess of roads is the goddess of the road through the heavens, the Milky Way (Vrou Elden Straat). The goddess Percht or Bertha (The White Lady, an aspect of Holda), keeps watch over the *heimchen*, shades of children who die in infancy, who watch over the growing plants, bringing them the nurturing dew. Her most active time is after midwinter. Like Frigg, Percht and Bertha is a patroness of spinning.

Another Germanic Frigg-like goddess is Gertrud: the female counterpart of Odin, Wode or Frau Gode, is the leading goddess of Asgardreia, the Wild Hunt. In Scotland, she is called Nincnevin.

Throughout Nordic and Celtic legend, men and women wishing to gain answers to questions, or to attain wisdom, visit wise women, giantesses and goddesses, from whom they obtain what they need. For instance, Svipdag consults his dead mother, the seeress Groa, in the underworld for advice.

The giantess magician Hyndla is visited by Freyja for information about the lineage of her human lover, Ottar. Odin, god of enlightenment, learns magical techniques from Freyja; through her trance-mediumship, he obtains the runes.

Grid loans her magic gloves, belt and staff to Thor when he visits the giant Geirrod, and Hyrrokin's strength is needed to push Balder's funeral ship out to sea. Giantesses, too, are the gods' lovers. Frey loves Gerda, whilst the wave-maiden Jarnsaxa is one of Thor's consorts. Thus, the female members of the pantheon's, far from being insignificant, symbolise almost every aspect of human and divine existence. Their sacred days are spread throughout the calendar.

After the fall of the Roman Empire in western Europe, the female divine principle, acknowledged by the Pagans, was driven gradually underground, forbidden by theocratic governments. Of course, this deterred only the external forms of Goddess-awareness, whilst leaving the inner, secret, core relatively unaffected.

Externally, the Goddess reasserted herself in the thirteenth century of the Common Era, when the worship of Mary, Mother of God became prominent in the western church. This was in response to the Crusaders' horror when they entered the Wasteland, the barren deserts of

North Africa and the Middle East, which, according to Arab mystics, had come into being as the result of renouncing the Goddess there.

The patriarchal, authoritarian cult of mastery, promoting the conquest of Nature, had destroyed the older, more nurturing, ecologically-sustaining, ways, replacing them with a destructive on-lay.

The salutary shock of encountering the Wasteland led to the setting-up of cults of more active female saints, themselves versions of female Pagan deities.

Later, the secession of the Protestants from the western church led to a renewed suppression of female aspects of the divine. Images of the Madonna and female (and male) saints were destroyed. In central and southern Europe, however, the Roman Catholic Counter-Reformation gave the Madonna even more prominence.

Many new shrines of the Mother of God were created, and the cult of the Black Madonna thrives today. Like the deserts of North Africa and the Middle East, the modern wasteland of industrial-military pollution has also come about through patriarchal theologies of command and control.

These preach the transformation of the world into a re-presentation of reality patterned in the image of Man - an on-lay that stems from the renunciation of the Goddess. It is important to note that this Industrial Revolution came out of Protestant countries, where the feminine principle of the Madonna had been driven out once again.

To the, the Earth was no longer sacred, but an object, a *'resource'* to be used for the short-term profit of individuals. The desacralized cosmos had arrived, and the program to make the Earth alfreka commenced. It is still continuing. The image of the Goddess, wherever she exists, is symbolic of the spiritual resistance to this.

The Madonna iconography of the Christians is a continuation of various Pagan depictions of the Goddess, especially from icons of Isis and late versions of the Ephesian Artemis or Diana. In his remarkable work, *Salammbo*, Gustave Flaubert describes a shrine of the goddess:

> *"They entered an apartment containing nothing except a black painting representing a woman. Her legs reached to the top of one of the walls; her body occupied the entire ceiling; from her navel hung, suspended by a thread, an enormous egg; and the remainder of her body, her head downward, descended the other wall, to the level of the pavement, where her finger ends touched".*

Coming from the Great Goddess, the titles of Our Lady; Mother of God, Queen of Heaven, and The Great Mother are those with which Artemis, Diana, Isis, Frigg and Brenhines-y-Nef were adored in antiquity.

In the Americas, she was assimilated with her equivalent West African goddess. Thus, in voudoun, she is Erzoulie Frieda Dahomey, otherwise known as Ezilie or Maitresse (The Lady), the personification of love and beauty, richness, wealth without limit and sublime luxury.

Erzoulie may be compared with Aphrodite and Freyja. She is the goddess who stands against disorder, bringing order out of chaos - *ordo ab cho*. In Brazilian Candomble, Our Lady is Iemanja, the mother of all the *orixas*, a beautiful and exulted archetype of spiritual motherhood.

Symbolically, the Madonna's blackness represents the fertility of the earth, the dark chthonic qualities that support and complement the bright, light qualities of male divinity. It is only through the convoluted, unconvincing pretexts of monotheistic dogma that she is not actually afforded her true status as the Goddess in the Christian sect.

However, many contemporary Pagans recognise that in the Catholic church, the goddess is recognised in the form of Our Lady. Thus, every shrine of Our Lady is a shrine of the Great Goddess, and is therefore worthy of veneration. The festivals of the year that acknowledge Our Lady in her various forms are also sacred in the Pagan view of existence.

Part Two:

The Goddess Year

January

amed after the two-faced Roman god Janus, the goddess of this month is Juno, who at this time of year is portrayed in a similar way. Her backward-looking aspect is called Postvorta, and her forward looking one, Antevorta.

These two-faced deities are the best known examples of what was in former times a widespread way of portraying divinity. The 'Janus-faced' goddesses and gods of the Celts are an important part of this tradition, though the multi-faced deities of the Baltic and Slav pantheon's are less well recognised in the west.

Apart from depicting the multivalent nature of the deities, the symbolism of this portrayal is of orlog, that everything which exists now still contains within itself that which is past. The possibilities which can take place in the new year are nevertheless dependent upon certain events that took place in the old one. This is the nature of the tension between continuity and creativity, innovation and tradition.

The Common Era Gregorian calendar used throughout Europe is based on the older Roman Pagan Julian calendar that was instituted by Julius Caesar. But this is not the only possible calendar we can use, for contemporary Pagans have a number of others that fit more appropriately to their spiritual systems.

They are the goddess calendar of *Lux Madriana,* used by members of the Fellowship of Isis, the Celtic tree calendar and the Runic time cycles of The Way of the Eight Winds.

The *Lux Madriana* goddess calendar dedicates its months to goddesses who stand as regents of their corresponding time-periods. It commences on *December 26th,* and hence it does not coincide completely with the Gregorian months or years of the Common Era. Until the *22nd,* the month of January is overlapped by the *Lux Madriana* month of Hestia. After this, the month of Brighde commences (until *February 19th*).

Simultaneously, with the typical strong pluralism of Pagan thought, we can measure the year in terms of alternative ways of viewing nature, in this instance, the Celtic tree-months. This calendar is based upon 18th century Irish bardic tradition, formalised by the inspired bard Robert Graves in his seminal book, *The White Goddess.*

The Celtic birch-tree month of Beth begins the Gregorian year. This rules until the *20th,* when it gives way on the *21st* to the rowan-tree month, Luis, whose deity is the Morrigan. In the runic time-system, the year is divided equally into 24 half-months, to each of which in order is assigned one of the runes of the elder futhark. The traditional sequence of the runes assigns their meanings to times of year whose qualities are remarkably consistent with their traditional meanings.

The full nature of this system is explained by the author in his *Runic Astrology* (Capall Bann, 1995). The month of January begins under the regency of the yew-tree rune, Eoh, whose power is changed on the *13th*, Tiugunde Day, to that of the rune Peorth. The womb-cup rune Peorth is itself superseded on *January 28th* by the half-month of the defensive and protective rune Elhaz.

January 1st

New Year's Day, la na bliadhn'ure, is sacred to the turning wheel-goddesses who are exemplified by Fortune (Lady Luck) and Arianrhod. This is a time of symbolic new beginnings and consequent uncertainty, for who knows what the new year will bring?

January 7th

Is sacred to the Egyptian lion-headed goddess Sekhmet, who, during the time of the Roman Empire, was worshiped as far north as the British Isles. Her image is known from the Temple of Mithras near Caernarfon in Wales, where she held a cross of iron. Thus, the goddesses of Egypt are as much part of British Paganism as the Celtic goddesses and gods and the later deities that came from Denmark and Germany with the Anglo-Saxons.

The eve of January 6th

Is the night of the goddess Percht, among other things, guardianness of the souls of unborn children. She is the most important goddess of Alsace, southern Germany, Austria, and Switzerland, and is honoured in the Perchtenlauf ceremonies.

Percht's night is a time of wonder, when animals speak and we make wishes that can be fulfiled. It is the time when we purify our homes, making pentagrams on doors, windows and beds. At this time, too, the three weird sisters are active.

The Goddesses of January 11th

Are the nine classical muses, and corresponding goddesses of the Celtic and Germanic pantheon's, and on the *16th*, the goddesses of harmony, such as the Roman Concordia and the Nordic Hlin, are remembered.

The next significant goddess-date is the *30th*, when the goddess of peace is honoured on the eve of Imbolc. In the Roman tradition, she is Pax, and in the Northern Tradition, Sif plays this part. As Ovid wrote in his *Fasti*:

> "*Come, Peace....and let your gentle presence live in the whole world. So if there are no enemies nor reasons for triumphs, to our generals you will be a greater glory than war. May the soldier bear arms only to deter the armed aggressor, and may the warlike trumpet sound only for solemn pomp! Priests, add incense to the fires that blaze on the altar of Peace!*"

Because of the örlog of our times, since the nineteenth century, people have not used the apparent position of the sun to measure the time of day. The natural time-cycles under the rulership of Frigg, Queen of Heaven, have been overridden by literalist machines. Instead, clocks, related to a fictitious 'mean time' have been the standard.

Unlike the strictly regular progress of the clock, the apparent motion of the sun is irregular. Because of this, solar and clock time at any one place only coincide four times a year: at other times, they are divergent. Added to this, the division of the world into time-zones means that if we are not on the corresponding meridian, then the time we tell from the clock will be considerably different from that by the sun, which is Real Time.

Full details of this important principle are explained in the author's *Runic Astrology* (Capall Bann, 1995).

By the mid-1990s, all of western Europe, except the British Isles, uses Central European Time, a clock based upon a meridian that runs through western Poland that is defined by the once-sacred island of Bornholm in the Baltic. Thus, the Real Time in Portugal, for instance, is, during the extra hour added to the clock for 'summertime', the best part of 3 hours behind the Central European Time on the clock. Clearly, this is absurd, yet it is normality!

Using the clock to plot, for instance, planetary hours for use in magical operations, is therefore useless. The equation of time enables us to calculate the difference between Real Time and local mean clock time.

On New Year's Day, apparent solar time is 3 minutes slow of the clock; by the *11th*, this is 8 minutes, and by the *21st*, 11 minutes. At the end of the month, Real Time is just over 13 minutes behind clock time.

February

ebruary is the month of the goddess Februa, usually seen as an aspect of Juno, who, as Juno Februa is mother of the god Mars, whose month comes next. In the Northern Tradition, she parallels Odin's consort, Frigg, and the goddess Brigid or Brigantia.

In the Celtic tree-calendar, the rowan-month of Luis runs until *February 17th,* followed on the *18th* by the ash-tree month, Nuin. In February, the runic half-month of Elhaz is superseded by the rune of solar power, Sigel, on the *12th.* This is regent of time until the *27th*, when the runic half-month of Tyr takes over.

The beginning of February falls the first major Pagan festival of the Gregorian year, the cross-quarter day known variously as Imbolc, Oimelc, la fheil Brigdhe nan cannlean, Gwyl Fair y Canhwyllan and Brigantia.

Although effectively in the middle of winter, and sometimes the coldest day of the year, this festival is taken to mark the beginning of the spring quarter of the year, when the darkness of midwinter is mitigated by increasing day-length.

This festival is sacred to the nine Disir, the shining goddesses, and the Celtic goddess, Brigantia, Brigida or Brigid, who appears in her Nordic form as Birgit. In mainland Europe, Brigida is the goddess of mountain passes, giving us the way through the otherwise impenetrable wintry alpine heights.

Here, at this time of year, Brigid symbolises the opening-out of enclosed, invisible nature concealed in the darkness of wintertide into the visible world of light. In the Irish tradition, she is a threefold goddess of fire-craft, poetry and healing. La fheil Brigdhe, St Brigid's Day, is celebrated in Ireland as one of the major festivals, assimilated with the Catholic observance of the festival of lights called Candlemas that originated in the old Pagan Lupercalia, celebrated on the *15th*.

At Brigid's shrine in Kildare, the sacred fire was tended by 19 women in a fenced enclosure into which no men were allowed to enter.

Having burnt continually under Paganism, Celtic Christianity and Catholic Christianity, it was extinguished finally by the order of the Archbishop of Dublin, Henry of London, in 1220.

The number 19 occurs in the cycle of the sun and moon, and in the number of stones in the Merry Maidens stone circle in Cornwall. The Candomble *orixa* Iemanja, goddess of harmony and happiness, mother of all the *orixas*, is venerated on the foreshore on *February 2nd* with offerings of flowers (especially roses) and perfume.

In contemporary Asatru, the Gregorian February is called Horning. *February 5th* is the day of the goddess of fortune, the Greek Tyche and the Roman Fortune. On *February 11th,* 1858, one of the most celebrated instances of an apparition of Our Lady was seen at Lourdes in France, which subsequently became a major place of pilgrimage and healing.

The Nordic love-goddess Sjofn is recalled on *February 14th* in the day dedicated to the shady saint, Valentine. As a month of love, February was personified by the Catholic church as St Febronia, who is the principle of *febris*, the fever of love.

February 15th is the festival of Lupercalia, commemorating the she-wolf who is the tutelary goddess of Rome and hence the whole Empire and its successors. In the north, it is the day of the wise women of the forests, the Vargamors of Swedish tradition, who not only ran with the wild wolves, but were the only people who were capable of a rapport with these ferocious beasts.

The Fornacalia, an old Roman festival of the goddess Fornax, held on *February 17th,* commemorates the oven in which our staple food, bread, is baked. *"The oven is the mother"* says the adage of the Fornacalia, whose close connection with fornication is no coincidence. Like January, the latter part of this month has few notable festival days.

Real Time in February begins around 13 and a half minutes slow of clock time. It remains around this greatest point of divergence for most of the month, being at about 14 and a half minutes between the *8th* and *16th*. By the end of the month, Real Time is 12 and a half minutes slow of mean clock time.

March

In the main western calendar, March is the month sacred to the god Mars, who in the Northern Tradition is Tyr or Termagant. This is apparent in the Irish name for the month, Mi an Mharta, the month of Mars. But Mars is not just a martial month.

Its Anglo-Saxon name, for example, expresses the female, nurturing aspect of springtime. It is called Hrethmonath, this means Hertha's Month, designating it as the time of year sacred to the Earth Mother goddess Hertha or Nerthus, for in March comes the vernal equinox. Thus, to the old English, March was seen as the month of springtime renewal.

This element of new growth is also commemorated in the old Frankish name for the month, Lentzinmanoth, which means 'renewal month'. Modern Asatru' calls March Lenting, an old Heathen name related to the Christian fast-period of Lent, which usually falls during some part of the month of March.

The Celtic ash-tree month of Nuin occupies the first part of the Gregorian month of March. On *March 18th*, this is superseded by the alder-tree month, Fearn. In Irish and

British tree-lore, the alder is a tree of protection against conflict, having the power to resist water and fire. According to the *Lux Madriana* goddess calendar, *March 19th* is the end of the month of Moura. It is followed on *March 20th* by the month of Columbina.

March 1st
Is the festival of the Matronalia, whose patroness is the goddess Juno Lucina, who parallels Frigg in her aspect as the patroness of married woman. In Roman Pagan observance, prayers were made to the goddess by women asking for good marriages. Women were given presents by the men, and flowers brought to the shrine of the goddess.

Also, on every *March 1st*, the fire of Vesta at Rome was re-kindled in the manner of the need-fire, by the friction of wooden members.

March 5th
Marks the ancient Egyptian festival of *Navigium Isis* (The Ship of Isis), in recognition of the goddesses invention of the sail, and her patronage of sailing in general. It is observed as the beginning of the new sailing season.

March 7th
Is the Junonalia, a festival observed by the Romans in honour of the goddess Juno. A procession of 27 girls, dressed in long robes, accompanied the image of the goddess, carved from the wood of the Cypress tree, which is sacred to her.

In the European Pagan calendar, *March 12th* is a solemn day of remembrance for the victims of religious persecution. Specifically, it commemorates an appaling act of religious intolerance that led to the martyrdom of Hypatia, known as The Divine Pagan.

Born in the year 370 CE, she was Dean of the Neoplatonic School at Alexandria. But simply because she was the most famous woman Pagan philosopher and mathematician of her time, she was kidnapped and murdered by a Christian mob whose members hated women, Pagans and philosophy.

The later medieval witch-hunts showed this institutionalised cruelty at its most horrific. Religious terrorism is not just a modern invention, and since those days vast numbers of others have died simply because of their religious beliefs. Two days after the festival of remembrance comes the start of the runic half-month of Beorc, a time-period whose regent is the white goddess of the Birch Tree. This half-month is symbolic of the purification necessary for any new beginnings.

The fateful Ides of *March 15th*, is best remembered as the day on which Julius Caesar was assassinated in BCE 44. But it is more than this, for it is simultaneously a number of sacred festivals.

Firstly, it is one of the holy days of Rhea, the Greek version of the Great Mother who is known otherwise as Cybele, and who, in the north, is paralleled by Fjorgynn, Nehalennia and Erda, the earth-goddess who gave us birth.

Anna Perenna, the nymph of the Italian River Numicius, was also revered on this day. Similarly, in Ireland, Anna Livia Plurabelle, the nymph who is a personification of the River Liffey that runs through Dublin, is also celebrated now. Her image can be seen and admired in the middle of O'Connell Street in that city. Similarly, the Candomble *orixa,* the goddess Oxum, is revered at running water. Generally, river sprites or nymphs should be acknowledged on the Ides of March.

March 19th
Is one of the festivals of the Greek goddess Athena, the Roman Minerva. In former times, on this day each year, the festival of the Lesser Panathenaea was celebrated.

A larger version of the festival, the Greater Panathenaea, was held every fifth year, and in the third year of every Olympiad. In Roman times, this day was celebrated as the festival of the birth of the goddess Minerva, called Quinquatrus.

The spring equinox, which usually falls around *March 20th -21st,* is one of the four Lesser Sabbats of wicca, known by its Druidic name of Alban Eilir.

According to the Fellowship of Isis, this is the festival of "The Resurrection of Our Lady", the commencement of the month of Columbina. Also, it is the day sacred to the Nordic goddess Iduna, who, as bearer of the magic apples of life that sustain the gods, personifies the light half of the year between the spring and autumnal equinoxes.

On this day, having been absent during the dark winter half of the year, she reappears in the form of a sparrow, bringing joy to all humans who see her flying through the air.

In Irish geomythic tradition, the holy city of Tara was founded on this day by the Milesian princesses Tea and Tephi. The vernal equinox is the fifth Station of the Year, the time of reconciliation when the seed, which for all appearances has been dead, miraculously comes back to life once more.

March 23rd
Is the Nordic festival known as Summer Finding that marks the beginning of the time of year when the light of the sun is more powerful than the darkness, that is, the summer half of the year.

March 24th
Is the holy day of the goddess Prytania or Britannia, symbolic spiritual embodiment of the Island of Britain, its guardianness and patroness of its bards.

Although she has been misrepresented often and is frequently overlooked, Britannia's power as guardian spirit of the land is still present.

The emblem of this country has always been and remains a Pagan goddess. This time of year has always been seen as a time of creation. According to third-century Christian texts, *March 25th* was thought of as being the actual date of the creation of the world by the demiurge. The treatise *De Pascha Computus*, written in the year 243 CE, states that the sun and moon were created on Wednesday, *March 28th*.

Before the adoption of *December 25th* as the 'correct' date (in the year 336 CE by the Catholics at Rome and 377 by the Orthodox at Constantinople).

March 28th was celebrated as the date of the nativity of Jesus of Nazareth. This was not without reason: for this day is the old Roman festival of The Sacrifice at the Tombs, when departed ancestors were remembered and honoured. In the Gregorian calendar, this day is observed as St Mark's Eve, a time of divination when the inscrutable Norns are a little more accessible than usual.

It is also the day on which, in 1802, the astronomer Olbers discovered the second known asteroid, which he named after the epithet of the goddess Athena, Pallas, whose festival falls in March.

March 30th

Marks the Roman Pagan festival of Janus and Concordia. It is the commencing-day of the runic half-month of Ehwaz, the horse-rune. This is a time of combination, partnership of humans with nature in the manner of the inseparable bond between rider and horse requiring mutual trust and loyalty.

This is a good time to begin a pilgrimage, either as a spiritual path or a physical journey. Real Time on this day is running only 4 and a half minutes behind clock time. On the last day of March is the Roman festival of Luna, whose moon-temple on the Aventine Hill was the focus of worship on this day.

The greatest British example of a moon temple is the Royal Crescent in Bath, which, although a terrace of fine houses, was designed by the Druidic architect John Wood the Elder in honour of the Moon.

Real Time on *March 9th* sees local mean clock time running 11 minutes earlier than Real Time. March is a period when Real Time rapidly comes much closer to clock time.

By *March 16th*, organic Real Time stands ten minutes behind local clock time, but on the vernal equinox it is only seven minutes behind the mechanical time of the clock.

April

The fourth month, April is named after the Greek goddess Aphrodite, who, in the *interpretatio Romana* is called Venus, and who is sometimes allied with the Nordic Frigg.

The poet Ovid called April

> *"the fourth month, in which thou art honoured above all others, and thou knowest, O Venus, that both the poet and the month are thine."*

April is called the season of *'opening'* because its name resembles the Latin word for *'open'*, *apertum*.

In April, the earth opens to receive seed and it is the time when the young leaves and blossoms of growing plants unfold and open up.

The Irish name for April, Aibrean, follows the Latin original, whilst to the Anglo-Saxons, this month was Eastermonth, the month sacred to the springtime goddess Eostre or Ostara, who in the *Interpretatio Nordmannicum* appears as an aspect of the Greek deity Aphrodite.

According to other ideas, she is the lunar goddess of the east. Similarly, the Franks named the month after the goddess of springtime, calling April Ostarmanoth. Likewise contemporary followers of the Asatru religion call it Ostara.

The first day of April is best known as All Fools' Day, the only day upon which it is socially permissible to play tricks and practical jokes on others - but only until Noon.
All Fools' Day is the archetypal Festival of Fools, where the conventions and norms of social life are turned round for a while, but still strictly under certain defined conditions.

In every stable society, in order that things should not become too rigid, there are periods when a certain amount of misrule is permitted for a short, well-defined, time.

April 1st

Is also the Roman women's festival of Fortune Virilis, in which the goddess Venus is invoked for good relations with men. According to the nineteenth century Irish writer Amlaoibh O Suilleabhain.

> "At the time when Venus was worshiped, the first day of the month was a festival in her honour, and it was customary to play all sorts of low pranks to do her veneration."

On *April 4th*, the ancients celebrated the Megalesia, the festival of the Great Mother, Cybele. In his *Fasti*, Ovid wrote:

"Right away, the Berecynthian flute will play a note on its curved horn, and the festival of the Idaean Mother will have come....

The goddess herself will be carried with cheering through the city streets...".

Another text states

"Thou fruitful Mother of the Gods, accept gratefully the prayers of thy devotee".

The festivities of the Great Goddess continued through the next six days, until *April 10th.*

Apꞅíl 11ᴄh

The festivities of the cereal-goddess, Ceres, commenced with games in her honour. The festival of the Cerealia proper began on the *11th,* and continued until *April 19th.* Ovid again:

"There is no need to state the reason (for the festival of Ceres); for the bounty and acts of the goddess are obvious. The bread of the first humans consisted of the green plants that the earth gave up without asking.....

Ceres was the first who invited mankind to better nourishment and exchanged the acorns for more wholesome food. She forced the bulls to offer their necks to the yoke; then, for the first time, the overturned soil beheld the sun.....

Ceres delights in peace; and you, the farmers, pray for unceasing peace and a conciliatory ruler. Give the goddess spelt, salt and grains of incense on ancient hearths; and of you have no incense, burn resin-full torches. Good Ceres is content with but a little, if that little be pure."

The Celtic alder-tree month of Fearn occupies the first half of April, ending on the *14th*. This is an important day in the North Sea region originating in Norse usage.

It is Summer's Day, the beginning of the summer half of the year, the day when it was safe in the days of sail to resume long-distance navigation. Summer's Day has its corresponding opposite, Winter's Day, Vinternatsblot, in October.

The Celtic tree-month of Fearn is followed on *April 15th* by the willow-tree month, Saille. This is also connected with sea-voyaging, for it is the month when the powers of Lady Moon are said to be at their greatest strength.

As ruler of the tides, it is necessary to acknowledge the Moon in all seafaring activities. *April 15th* is one of the days when we acknowledge the Earth Mother, who in ancient Italy was called Tellus Mater. Her feast was observed by the Vestal Virgins.

Today, every aspect of the Earth Mother is celebrated on *April 15th*. In the *Lux Madriana* calendar of the Fellowship of Isis, the month of Columbina occupies the Gregorian month of April until the *17th*, after which the month is dedicated to Maia commences.

April 23rd

Is best known in England as St George's Day, who in folk-tradition is personated as the Green Man. This is also a special day in Baltic Paganism, when the deity Latinized as Pergrubius was acknowledged at the festival of Jore. To classical Pagans, this is the festival of the Vinalia Priora, in honour of the divinity of Venus. Ovid tells us to

> *"Offer her incense and pray for beauty and popular favour; pray that you might be charming and witty; give to the queen her own myrtle and the mint that she loves, and bunches of rushes concealed in clusters of roses".*

April 28th

Is the festival of the spring time flower-goddess, Flora, to whom prayers are offered for fine growth and abundance of fields and trees. The Floralia, her festival was instituted in 238 BCE. Men were decked in roses, whilst women wore their finest dresses. Together, they celebrated with joy. The British flower-goddess Blodeuwedd is honoured today as the local manifestation of Flora.

After sunset on the last day of April comes May Eve, known in German-speaking lands as Walpurgisnacht. This is the festival of St Walpurgis, who is believed by many wiccans to be the Christianisation of a Germanic Earth Mother goddess, Walburg. European literature associates many of the dark goddesses with this time. They are very eclectic, coming from every source which has had influence within the European sphere. In his *Faust*, Goethe mentions Lilith, illustrated here, in connection with Walpurgis Night.

The relationship between local mean clock time and Real Time in April is balanced. At the beginning of the month, it is running just under 4 1/4 minutes slow, getting closer and closer until on the *16th*, Real Time and clock time coincide for one of the four times in the year when this happens. Passing through this node, by the end of the month, 4 minutes fast of clock time.

May

The Merry Month of May is named after the goddess Maia or Majestas, who is the most senior of the Greek Pleiades, or Seven Sisters.

According to ancient Greek religion, Maia was the mother of the messenger of Olympus, Hermes, who himself bestowed his mother's name upon the fifth month of the year. In the *Interpretatio Romana,* Roman Paganism identified her with the ancient Italian goddess of spring, Maia Majestas.

The Irish Celtic queen, Medb or Maeve can be seen as a northern incarnation of this goddess. Later, in the works of William Shakespeare, the Celtic queen became the fairy Queen Mab. Her sacred plant, the Hawthorn, or May tree, blossoms during this month, which is a time of most vigorous growth.

This is recognised in the Old English name for the month, Sproutkale, a name that evokes visions of luxuriant plant growth.

The old Frankish name for the Merry Month is Winnemanoth, the joy-month, that expresses our pleasure at the oncoming summer, as likewise does the contemporary Asatru month-name, Merrymoon.

The runes that rule the Merry Month of May are the stave of growth and flow, Lagu, whose half-month begins on *April 20th*. The attributes of this time-period are of vigorous, energetic, growth.

On May 14th
Lagu is followed by the runic half-month of Ing, which promotes the virtues of fertility and procreation. This rune is regent of time until *May 28th*.

On May 29th
The half-month of Odal begins. This is the half-month of immutable, ancestral property, the maintenance of the land and customs that define us as what we are.

As the beginning of summertime, the Merry Month of May is the period when the joys of spring and summer are manifested. These take the form of the ceremonies of Maying and the traditional love games of May Day.

As the first day of Summer, May Day is one of the four cross-quarter days of the natural calendar. May Eve is one of the three *ysbryndnos* (spirit nights) of Welsh tradition, the other two being St John's Eve (Old Midsummer) and Nos Galan Gaeaf (Hallowe'en).

In the Welsh tradition, May Day is Calan Mai (the calends of May), or Calan Haf (the calends, or beginning of summer). To contemporary Pagans, May Day is Beltane, a version of which is the current Irish name for the Merry Month of May, Mi an Bhealtaine.

In Irish, May Day itself is La Bealtaine. The name Beltane refers to the custom of lighting a bonfire, from the Irish word for fire, *taine*. This bonfire, called in Welsh, *coelcerth,* should be composed of nine types of wood, the nine sacred trees of British Pagan tradition.

The first part of Beltane's name comes from the solar god 'Beel' or 'Bal', who appears in the Northern Tradition in the form of the gods Beli, Belinus and Balder, of whom the goddess Anna is consort. According to the mystic cycle, Beltane is the sixth Station of the year, whose attribute is mystical union.

The sexual unions traditional in the *pleasaunce* of Maying are sacred because the man and woman are at that time personifications of the god and goddess. On May Day, the Maypole, symbolic of the *Phallus Dei* is planted in the womb of the Earth Mother symbolising the mystic marriage of opposites.

Although Maypole traditions flourish undimmed in German-speaking countries, in Great Britain we are not so fortunate, for the venerable Pagan tradition was attacked ruthlessly by religious fanatics during the sixteenth and seventeenth centuries. Then, much was erased from folk-tradition, remaining in many places as a mere memory. But May day was formerly the epitome of 'Merrie England', as celebrated by William Fennor in his 1619 work, *Pasquil's Palinodia:*

"When no capricious Constable disturb them,
Nor Justice of the Peace did seek to curb them
Nor peevish Puritan, in railing sort,
Nor over-wise Church Warden spoiled the sport;
Happy the age, and harmless were the days
(For then true love and amity were found),
When every village did a Maypole raise,
And Witson Ales and May-games did abound."

Traditionally, May is a particularly favoured month for the appearance on Earth of goddesses, and her apparitions are often seen around this time. In the evening of *May 3rd,* Bona Dea, the Good Goddess who presides over women's mysteries, is honoured.

In ancient Rome, the goddesses mysteries were celebrated in secret through this night by the Vestal Virgins. In the temples where observances took place, all male images were covered with a veil, whilst rooms were decorated with vine branches and flowers.

May 4th
That follows is the day that the whitethorn or hawthorn tree is honoured. This widespread and useful thorn-tree is the sacred plant of the goddesses at this time of year. This festival is known as The Veneration of the Thorn, which is marked by making offerings of prayer, music, food and ribbons to holy bushes and trees, such as those marking sacred places and guarding holy wells. The Christianised female deity of this day is known as St Monica.

May 9th

Is the first day of the Roman festival called the Lemuria. This is the time that the lemures, the wandering spirits of dead, are remembered. The lemures are dead family members who revisit their former homes on this day. The shades are acknowledged on the three days of the Lemuria, for the other two days when the spirits are abroad are *May 11th* and *13th*. This is the time when the hungry ghosts in houses and gardens must be fed if problems with them are to be averted.

The first half of May is paralleled by the Celtic willow-tree month of Saille. Saille ends on *May 12th*, and on the *13th*, the whitethorn-month, huath commences, bringing, like its thorny symbol, sure pro⋯ion of the inner and outer realms.

In the year 1917, *May 13th* saw the celebrated and enigmatic apparition of Our Lady at Fatima in Portugal, which was one of the notable of a series of apparitions of goddesses which has taken place in Europe during the twentieth century.

May 14th

Sees the beginning of the runic period under the regency of the rune Ing. This is the god Ing, the male consort of the Earth Mother goddess, Nerthus. Ing is god of the hearth, and his rune is the symbol of light, the firebrand or beacon that spreads its light far and wide.

This time of year expresses the energy-potential of summer, and its capability of almost limitless growth.

May 15th

Is the day on which the goddess of the month, Maia, her son, Mercury and also the goddess Vesta, are honoured. On this day, the Vestal Virgins conducted a rite for their tutelary goddess, Vesta, divinity of the hearth and eternal fire. This ceremony was intended to regulate the water supply for the coming summer. The *Lux Madriana* month of Maia occupies the first half of the Gregorian month of May. It ends on *May 15th,* being followed by the month dedicated to Hera.

May 17th

Brings the observance of the day of Dea Dia, the Great Mother Goddess, who, according to some contemporary goddess worshippers honour her this day in her aspect as the cosmos, space as the mother of matter.

May 23rd

Comes the feast of the Rosalia, which is a rose festival in honour of the goddess Flora. On the next day, the Floralia is followed by the observance of the festival of the Matron's or Mothers, *Y Mamau* in the Welsh Bardic tradition. These three goddesses are very important in the Celtic religion. At Arles in Provence in the south of France, the Mothers are celebrated in their guise as the Three Marias of the Sea at a pilgrimage attended by Romani people from all over Europe.

The Roman festival of the Ambarvalia was celebrated on *May 29th*, which is Oak Apple Day in England, in which the oak tree, sacred tree of the Druids and Druidesses, is venerated by the wearing of oak leaves.

The Ambarvalia is the festival of purification that was held in honour of two goddesses, Ceres and the Dea Dia, which was observed in ritual walking around fields of growing crops, thereby gaining divine favour for the growing plants.

The runic half-month of *Odal* begins today. This rune signifies ancestral property, the homestead, and all those things which are *"one's own"*.

The final day of the month of May is again dedicated to the goddess Frigg, in her aspect as mistress of the maytree or cosmic axis, Queen of Heaven.

On the first May, Real Time is running 2 and a half minutes in front of clock time. By *May 11th*, Real Time is actually four minutes early of clock time, and it remains about this point until the *20th*, when again it begins to approach clock time once more. Around the *25th*, Real Time is 3 and a half minutes *'fast'* of clock time, and by the end of the month, this has dropped to 2 and a half minutes.

June

The month of June is the time of the longest days in the year, for the midsummer solstice, the high point of the year, takes place around *June 21st.*

Midsummer's Day is known in the calendar of the Bards of the Island of Britain (the Druidic tradition) as Alban Hefin. In the Anglo-Saxon tradition, it is called Litha, and in the contemporary Lithuanian Romuva Paganism, Rasa.

Alban Hefin is the longest day of the year, which means that the sun remains above the horizon for the longest time, having risen and setting at its most northerly points.

Alban Hefin is the seventh Station of the year, the time of sanctification, when the flower opens and is fertilised. In this aspect, it is sacred to the goddess Cerridwen and the flower-maiden, Blodeuwedd.

Commemorating this, the former Druidic observance of midsummer sunrise at Stonehenge each year was suppressed by the authorities in 1987, thereby preventing adherents of the Elder Faith from visiting one of the major sacred places of European Paganism. But the tradition of hailing the sun at midsummer continues as it ever has at other sacred places of the sun.

Once called Junonius, the month of June is named after Juno, the Roman Great Mother goddess, who in the *Interpretatio Romana* is identified with the Greek goddess Hera, and again, in the Northern Tradition equivalent to Frigg and her various subsidiaries.

The female consort of the supreme deity, Jupiter, the goddess Juno is primarily the Queen of Heaven, an attribute that is given to a goddess in each European pantheon. In the Northern Tradition, for instance, the Queen of Heaven is Frigg, Odin's consort, whilst Mary, Our Lady in the Christian pantheon carries the identical attribute.

As Queen of Heaven, Our Lady performs the same function as Juno and Frigg, being the regent of the highest part of the year, midsummer, which is the time when there is the most light and the least darkness.

In Roman religion, the goddess Juno watches and guards the members of the female gender, and so form the woman's perspective, her month of June is considered be the most favourable one in which to marry.

Because June is the time of the longest day, and the brightest light, by there law of correspondences, symbolically it is the most auspicious month in which one may gain wealth. On a human level, this wealth is not so much money and material possessions, but possession of oneself, the attainment of the fullest development of the human being.

June 21st

Is celebrated in the goddess year as the day of all Heras or Junos. A Hera or Juno is a woman who, in her life here on earth has attained the fullest expression of her potential, which is full communion with the Mother of All Things, becoming a living embodiment of the Goddess on earth.

The Irish name of June is Meitheamh, whilst in modern Asatru it is called Fallow, the time when the hay is ready. According to the Nameless Art, the month of June is known as The Door of the Year. In spiritual terms, June is an entrance through which the inner realms may be entered. Thus, the rune which is the regent of the middle of June, is Dag, the rune of opening.

It signifies the good door, that which serves to exclude bad and harmful things whilst admitting only those things that are of benefit to us. Carna, the Roman goddess of door-hinges is revered on *June 1st*. Carna is primarily the goddess of the home and of family life, who therefore guards the main entrance of the house, letting in only those who should enter, and keeping out those who must not.

In the Northern Tradition, this function is taken by the includer-and excluder-goddess Syn. When one lives according to the principles of the magical house, then it is customary to attend to the maintenance of doors and windows on *June 1st*, because it is the day when Tempestas, the storm-goddess, must be remembered and acknowledged. The day is also sacred to Hebe, the cup-bearing goddess, whose attribute resembles the cauldron of the Celtic goddess Cerridwen, whose rites are celebrated at midsummer.

June 13th

Is the first of three holy days dedicated by the Guild of Flute-Players to the worship of the Roman goddess of war and healing, Minerva, who in Britain was assimilated with the the healing-goddess of the hot springs of Bath, Sul, as Sulis Minerva.

Her image can be seen today among the remains of her great temple at Bath, where the hot waters continue to issue from the earth, but, in which inexplicably, we are not permitted to bathe. Just as at Stonehenge, the sacred powers of Bath are kept from their proper use by those who cannot or will not understand the nature of sacred observance. It is up to all followers of the Elder Faith to keep up the pressure to change this situation, looking forward to the time when our sacred shrines are no longer desecrated, but are venerated once again.

The Northern Tradition Valkyries are remembered on this day of women's power. This day is also celebrated as the Nativity of the Muses, the nine daughters of Mnemosyne and Zeus, who symbolise the arts and sciences that bring utility and ornament to human life.

June 15th

The women of the Roman Empire celebrated their festival of first fruits, the Vestalia, which is sacred to the goddess Vesta and which was presided over by members of the college of priestesses of the goddess, the Vestal Virgins.

The Emperor Julian the Blessed, restorer of Roman Paganism after it had been persecuted by Christian emperors, died on this day in the year 363 and was elevated immediately to the pantheon.

As one of the major points of the turning of the wheel of the year, the vicinity of the solstice contains the sacred day of Fors Fortune, sacred to the goddess Fortune, Lady Luck, who holds the wheel of fortune. Her day is *June 24th*. Under the guise of the Christian festival of John the Baptist, Fortuna's day is the official Midsummer's Day of the British government.

The eve of this day is one of the three *ysbrydnos*, or spirit nights, in the Welsh tradition, the other two being May Eve and halloween. Like Christmas Day, which once was but no longer is the winter solstice, official midsummer is also awry of the true solstice, owing to the drift of the calendar away from the real solar phenomena upon which it is based.

It is customary to burn midsummer bonfires on high points on this day, especially on rock surfaces. In the *Lux Madriana* calendar, the *24th* is Rosea 12, Rosa Mundi, the Rose of the World, The Mother's Festival on which roses are given to the participants in the festival in which we meditate upon our relationship to our mothers and to the great mother of all, the heart of creation. *June 27th* is the old Roman festival of Initium Aestatis,the beginning of summertime in the Roman tradition. Regent of this time is the goddess of summer, Aestas.

In the Celtic annual cycle, the hawthorn month of Huath ends on *June 9th*. It is followed on *June 10th* by the oak-month, Duir, which reflects the runic month as a time of empowerment. Duir also signifies the door of the year that opens to admit good things.

Finally, according to the *Lux Madriana* calendar used by the Fellowship of Isis, the first twelve days of June are the final days of the goddess month of Hera, followed on *June 13th* by the rose-month dedicated to the goddess Rosea.

In the runic year-cycle, June is at the beginning. The first runic half-month, that begins with the powers of wealth and abundance, is ruled by the rune Feoh. It commences on *June 29th*, on which day our culinary and medicinal herbs are at their most potent, and must be harvested.

The first rune is sacred to the god and goddess Frey and Freyja, who are the Lord and Lady of certain branches of contemporary Wicca. Representing the collecting-together of power in whatever form it may take, this is the half-month of wealth and success. In her monetary aspect as Juno Moneta, the goddess was guardianness of money and wealth. In the city of Rome, on the Capitoline Hill, Juno's temple contained the mint where the coinage was manufactured.

Real Time in June is close to that of the clock. On *June 1st* is 2nd minutes *'fast'* of clock time, whilst on the *8th*, it is just over one minute *'fast'* of clock time.

It is on the *14th* that the equation of time brings together clock time and Real Time, one of only four times in the year when the mechanic time of the clock is in harmony with the organic time of the sun. Then there is no difference between local apparent noon and noon in local mean time. But nothing in nature is static, and *June 22nd* sees Real Time standing at 1 and a half minutes later than clock time.

July

This month is not named after a goddess, for it commemorates the Roman dictator Julius Caesar, under whose direction the chaotic Roman calendar was reformed and renamed the Julian calendar. This was implemented in the year 46 BCE, becoming the main calendar for the later Roman Empire and wider Europe. It formed the primary calendar of Europe, in both the Christian and Pagan parts, until the sixteenth century, when it was modified by Pope Gregory to become the present Gregorian calendar.

July 4th

Is the first significant day of the goddess in the month, dedicated to Pax, the Roman personification of peace in goddess form. This is followed on *July 7th* by the festival of Feriae Ancillarum, the Festival of Handmaids. In Roman Paganism, this was a sort of women's festival of fools, the maids' holiday on which they had license to do almost anything they chose.

On this day, devotees of Juno celebrated the feast of Nonae Caprotinae, where they partook of a ritual meal at her sacred tree, the fig.

Feriae Ancillarum is followed on the 8th by the day of the Christianised sun goddess in the Northern Tradition, Sol. She is the continuation of the Norse solar maiden, Sunna.

In northern Europe, most of the solar deities are female, from the Lithuanian goddess Saule in the east to the East Anglian Phoebe in the west. Counteracting the previous festival of light, *July 10th* is the festal day of Holda, Hela, and Skadi, three of the northern European goddesses of the shades and the underworld.

The ruling symbol of this day is the scythe, tool of the reapers who cut the hay, but also emblematic of the grim reaper, who is the scathing destroyer-goddess Skadi. Allied to her is the fabulous Celtic teacher of the martial arts, Scathach, to whose warrior-school at Dunscaith on the Isle of Skye came the men of the north to learn the body-knowledge necessary for those who take up the way of the fighting arts.

July 11th
Commences the Goddess month of Kerea, whilst on the *14th,* the runic half-month of Ur begins. The meaning of this rune is primal strength, signifying a time of collective strength, when 'our' power as a society can be best applied to projects for the common good.

July 15th
Is the day of the Olympic New Year. In northern Europe, it is sacred to the rowan-tree goddess, Rowana or Rauni. She is the patroness of the secret knowledge of the runes, saviour of Asa-Thor when he was swept away by a river.

In the Roman tradition, *July 23rd* sees the festivals of Neptunalia and Salacia. The first one celebrates the god Neptune, whilst the second is dedicated to the veneration of the goddess Salacia, who rules over the open, saline sea. Inland, she is the deity who rules over springing, highly-mineralised waters.

Sul, tutelary goddess of the hot springs at Bath is an aspect of Salacia. In the *interpretatio Nordmannicum*, the Roman divinities are equivalent to the sea-god and goddess Aegir and Ran.

July 25th
The goddess Furrina was celebrated in the festival called Furrinalia, Furrina is an ancient Italian goddess of freshwater springs, which may begin to dry up at this time of year in hot summers. Held two days after the Salacia, the Furrinalia completes the acknowledgement of the vital place that springs, of both sweet and mineral waters, hold in human life.

The goddess known as Bona Dea, the Good Goddess, is revered on *July 26th* as St Anna or St Anne. She is venerated in Candomble as Nanan, the grandmother Vovo, the oldest *orixa* of all. In northern Europe she is the goddess Nana, goddess of immaculate purity, wife of Balder and mother of Forseti. The Bona Dea was assimilated in the *interpretatio Romana* with the Celtic goddess Anna, who with her male consort Beli or Beel, the deity we acknowledge at Beltane, is the ancestress of all people of Celtic descent.

Several ancient Welsh genealogies, such as those of Coel Godebog, Rhodri the Great, St Beuno, St Catwg and St

David, traced back their forebears to Anna, sister or cousin of the Christian Virgin Mary. This is clearly a Christian reading of the principle of tracing royal or aristocratic genealogies back to a founding divinity.

The *Glossary* of Bishop Cormac, written in Ireland in the ninth century, states:

> "*Ana is Mater Deorum Hibernensium, well she used to nourish the Gods, from whose name is said Anae, i.e. abundance...as Anna was mother of the gods, so Buannann was mother of the Fiann...*"

In Brittany, several Pagan images of the Bona Dea are still revered in ch   .s under the name of St Anna. Even her images, showing her holding two babies, were copied for St Anne. Similarly, certain German images show a threefold Anna, emphasising her status as the mother goddess.

The dedication of St. Ann was applied to traditional holy wells, such as that at Whitstone in Cornwall, and that at Sneinton, Nottingham, where it was associated with the turf labyrinth that was finally destroyed in 1797.

The final goddess commemorated in July is Sigyn, consort of the Nordic trickster-god Loki. Unlike her husband, known for his deviousness, Sigyn is the paragon of constancy, standing by him in his self-made troubles and protecting him in the underworld, though he is bound in unbreakable fetters.

Like its English name, the month's Irish name, Iuil, comes from Julius. Contemporary Asatr' calls July Haymoon. The Celtic oak-month Duir has its last day on *July 7th*. Commencing the next day is the holly-month, Tinne, a month of balance, when the continuing flourishing growth of the vegetation continues with the shortening of the days towards autumn.

In this Gregorian month, the parallel Goddess calendar sees the end of the month of Rosea on *July 10th*, followed on *July 11th* by Kerea. Clock time in July is running in front of the sun.

July 6th

Real Time is 4 and a half minutes later than clock time, and by the *13th* it is 5 and a half minutes behind clock time.

The *20th* sees Real Time running six minutes behind the clock, whilst Real Time on *27th* is running 6 and a half minutes behind the clock.

Solar time remains more or less at this point for the rest of the month, until just after Lammas Day, when it begins to come nearer yet again to clock time.

August

ike July, August is named after an ancient Roman leader. This month commemorates the first Roman emperor, Augustus Caesar, who was elevated to the pantheon as restorer and reformer of Roman Paganism, which shortly before his time had fallen into decline.

The deity who rules the month of August is the goddess of harvest, Demeter, Ceres, Cerridwen or Sif, fitting for the harvest month.

According to the myth, the goddess Demeter left her original abode, Olympus, the abode of the divine, and dwells on Earth amongst us humans as other gods and goddesses are believed to have done.

The Gregorian month of August commences with the cross-quarter day known as Lammas. Most contemporary Pagans in English-speaking countries know it by the name Lughnassadh (pronounced loonasa), which is the unreformed spelling of the modern Irish month-name, Lunasa.

The Irish name of festival day of Lammas itself is La Liunasd. Whatever we call it, this month is named after the god of wisdom, Lugh, and his earthly manifestation, king Lugad of the Tuatha de Danaan, founder of the Telltown fair that commemorated his foster-mother, Tailltu.

In addition to Tailltu, the goddesses of this time, probably real women elevated to the pantheon, are the Machas of Ireland. Like many symbolic female figures, Macha is threefold. They are Macha, consort of Nemed; Macha, wife of Crunnchu; and Macha the Red.

The last Macha is the legendary queen also known as *'Macha of the Golden Hair'*, a name that symbolises her connection with the golden wheat, barley, spelt and oats that is harvested at Lammas. Rhiannon, *'The Great Queen'* is also honoured at this time of year.

Lammas is the festival of the First Harvest, when traditionally the first grain is gathered in, it is ground in the mill and then baked into the first loaf of the new grain. It is this loaf that we offer to Mother Earth in thanks for her continued grace towards us as human beings who live upon her, for her beneficent qualities and virtues are most apparent during this time of harvest.

The August festival of Lammas is the eighth and last Station of the year, the time of completion. Appropriately, in modern Asatr', this is the month called Harvest. The ancient Pagan Irish charge known as *The Lammas Assembly* tells us of the things which are appropriate to Lammastide:

132

"Heaven, Earth, Sun, Moon and Sea,
Fruits of Earth and Sea-stuff,
Mouths, ears, eyes, possessions,
Feet, hands, warriors' tongues."

The greatest Lammas Assembly of Ireland was a fair formerly held at Tailtenn, the sacred place of Tailltiu, known widely by its English name of Telltown, which is located on the river Blackwater between Navan and Kells. Here, traditional games were played and marriages celebrated.

The marriages took place in the Pagan *'common law'* manner, without Christian clergy or government officials, and were valid for one year. If the marriage did not work, then the couple returned after a year, and walked away from one another, divorced. If the marriage was a success, they left together after the fair. The last state Lammas fair held at Telltown was in the year 1169 in the presence of Roderick O'Conor, High King of Ireland.

This time of year, when the decline of day length is becoming noticeable, has several festivals of fire and light. Firstly, in England, *August 6th* is the traditional day of the Tan Hill festival, commemorating the personified Celtic holy fire, known as *teinne.*

August 12th

Is the ancient Egyptian festival of the Lychnapsia, otherwise The Lights of Isis, on which the goddess was seen as seeking Osiris in the darkness by torchlight. In its later, Christian, form, the Lychnapsia became the day of St Clare, who is the personification of the Holy Lights of the Goddess.

August 13th

Lights played a great part in the observance of a festival of the goddess Hecate, the Roman Diana. It was the slaves' holiday in ancient Rome, and women whose prayers to the goddess had been answered went in torchlit procession to Diana's temple at Aricia. There, the aid of the goddess was invoked to avert any autumnal storms that might destroy the coming harvest. On this day, too, the runic half-month of As begins. It is the time most sacred to the deities of Asgard, the goddesses and gods of stability and order.

At this time, we can be more aware of the divine forces that are at work in the world. Next comes another festival of women's lights, for *August 15th* is the day of St Mary.

She, as the continuation of the Great Mother Goddess in her fertile aspect, is is evoked to ensure a good vintage:

> *"On St Mary's Day, sunshine,*
> *Brings much good wine".*

As the major Christian festival of the Assumption of the Virgin Mary, it continues the practice of Pagan antiquity by using lights to celebrate the apotheosis of a human being into a goddess.

For Christian mythology tells how Mary was taken up to heaven bodily at the age of 75 on a day formerly reserved for the worship of Diana. Maria thus became Queen of Heaven in the Christian pantheon, a position recognised in the Orthodox church around the year 600, and about half a century later by the Catholic Church in the west.

August 23rd

Is the day of the goddess Nemesis, defender of the sacred in all its aspects, avenger of those whose tombs and bones are profaned by the sacrilegious or ignorant. The festival of the Nemesia acknowledges that the sacred must be maintained if society is not to disintegrate. Allied to her is Moira, the guardianness of personal destinies.

When we evaluate our lives on this day, we acknowledge her, and ask her aid in making and keeping resolutions for our future. Ops, the ancient Italian goddess of sowing and reaping is honoured on *August 25th*. In Roman Paganism, this was the festival known as the Opeconsiva. As goddess of the earth, with the title of Lady Bountiful the Planter, we should worship her in the traditional manner by sitting on the ground.

According to Egyptian tradition, *August 27th* is the day on which the goddess Isis came into being, and is thus the festival of the Nativity of Isis. In Roman times, London had the largest known temple of Isis north of the Alps, and so as Isis has been worshipped in Britain for longer than the Anglo-Saxon deities.

The next day follows with the related festival of the Nativity of Nephthys, the Egyptian equivalent of Aphrodite. Following this, *August 29th*, is the day on which devotees of Egyptian religion celebrated the nativity of the goddess Hathor.

It is also on this day that the runic half-month of Rad commences, signifying a rejoicing in motion, fertility and success, the channelling of energies in the correct manner to produce the desired results.

The holly-month of the Celtic tree-calendar, called Tinne, ends on August 4th. It is followed by the hazel-month called Coll, which is a time of gathering fruitfulness, both in the literal sense of harvest and more symbolically in the use of words as the power to express and use creative energies.

In the Goddess calendar, the month of Kerea occupies August until the *8th*, when it is followed by the month of Hesperis. The calendar of ancient Alexandria, from which Julius Caesar's Egyptian and Greek astronomers drew up the Julian Calendar, has its New Year's Day on *August 29th*.

August 3rd

Sees Real Time standing at just less than six-and-a-half minutes '*slow*' of clock time, whilst on the *10th*, Real Time is 5 and a half minutes 'slow' of the clock. The *17th* shows Real Time is running 5 minutes behind clock time. By *August 31st*, Real Time is only a few seconds '*slow*' of clock time.

September

eptember is named after the Latin *septem*, the number seven, because in the old Roman calendar, it was the seventh month. The names of the three following months, October, November and December also bear old Roman month numbers, eight, nine and ten respectively.

For Pagans, the most important day in September is the autumnal equinox, called Mabon in the Celtic tradition and Winter Finding in Asatru. It falls around *September 23rd.*

The Gregorian September is the Irish month of Mean Fomhair To modern Asatr', it is the month of Shedding, whilst in the tradition of East Anglia, this autumnal month is known as Barleysel, after the barley harvest. The Celtic hazel-tree month of Coll ceases on the first of September. Then, from the second until *September 29th* comes the vine-month called Muin.

Then, another Celtic month finishes the Gregorian month of September. It is the ivy-month of Gort which starts on *September 30th.*

This month is sacred to the goddess Brigid, being a period during which favourable aspects of the self may develop. It is a period of time when the individual may see beyond the everyday world into that which lies within and beyond. Like the climbing ivy, the month of Gort signifies the spiral-like ascent of the human spirit from the earthly, material plane of Abred into the world of enlightenment, Gwynvyd, the White Land.

The first part of September is ruled by the runic half-month of Rad, which on the *13th* is superseded by the time of Ken, the rune that signifies the light of the flaming torch. The half-month of Ken is the time-period when the creative fire of the forge, through the agency of human consciousness and acquired skills, enables us to transmute natural materials into something new that reflects in its structure the human intellect.

Ken signifies the mystical creation of a third thing which formerly did not exist, from the union of and transmutation of two others. The positive aspects of sexuality immanent in the goddess Freyja and the god Frey are brought into strong presence at this time.

Finally, *September 28th* is the beginning of the runic half-month of Gyfu. The Gyfu rune denotes the state of unity that a gift brings between the donor and the recipient. It is a time of unification, both between the members of society and the human and the divine. According to the *Lux Madriana* calendar the goddess month of Hesperis runs until *September 5th,* when it yields to the month dedicated to Mala.

September 2nd

The beginning of the Celtic vine-month of Muin, is the time of ingathering, the harvest-period when the raw materials of life, both on the physical and spiritual level, have been collected together so that we can process them into something useable on the human level. *September 8th* is dedicated to the Mother goddess in the shape of Our Lady, whose birthday this is.

September 13th

Is the Roman festival of the Lectisternia in which the three Capitoline Deities of Rome were acknowledged. Instituted in 399 BCE by the Sibylline Oracles, the Lectisternia comprised a ceremony in honour of Jupiter, Juno and Minerva, and then the Plebeian Games were held.

Around the *22nd* falls the autumnal equinox, which in the Druidic tradition is celebrated as of Alban Elfed. This equinox is the second Station of the Year, which is the time of calling or summoning, the ripening of the seed, which is the prelude to its release at the time of awakening at Samhain in November.

To some contemporary Pagans, the autumnal equinox is the festival of Mabon, which to the followers of Asatr' is the holy day of Winter Finding.

September 28th

Is the sacred day of the Swabian goddess Zisa, whose shrine, Zizarim, was at the present city of Augsburg in Germany. *September 30th* is the medical festival of Medetrina, the Roman goddess of medicines and healing.

Her counterparts, the Irish goddess Airmed and the Nordic Eir, are revered now with offerings of fruit.

In September, Real time crosses over clock time from being half a minute behind it on the first, to ten minutes *'fast'* by the end of the month.

On *September 2nd*, Mean local clock time is the same as local apparent time by the sun. *September 7th* sees Real Time being just over a minute *'fast'* of clock time, whilst, by the *14th* it is 4 minutes in advance of the clock. On *September 21st*, Real Time is almost seven minutes fast of the clock, and this discrepancy increases until it reaches its maximum divergence around *November 3rd..*

October

ctober, one of the *number months*, named as the eighth month of the old Roman calendar, is sacred to the goddess Astraea. She was the daughter of Zeus and Themis, who lived among humans during the Golden Age. But, when civilisation began to degenerate, she withdrew to the upperworld, leaving the earth to its own devices.

Symbolic of the departure of paradise or the Golden Age, the character of the goddess Astraea reflects the qualities of this month when the autumnal declining light and progressively colder nights indicate unequivocally that the golden age of summertime is past now, and that now things are in decline, and that the dark, cold, wintertime approaches rapidly.

October is the ancient Greek month of Demetryon, sacred to Demeter, for during this month, the last of the harvests can be gathered in.

In Ireland, the Gregorian month of October is called Deireadh Fomhair, whilst modern Asatru calls the month Hunting.

In the Celtic tree-calendar, the ivy-month known as Gort, occupies October until the *27th*, when it is followed on the *28th* by the reed-month Ngetal.

The reed is a symbol which expresses the power to gain knowledge, endowing us with the ability to discover order in the unknown, bringing inner transformation. During the tree-month of the reed, the forces of sun and moon are said to be in unison.

In the runic year-cycle, the first part of October is under the regency of the rune Gyfu, representing the unity of donor and recipient that comes from the act of giving.

October 13th
The half-month of Wyn commences. This denotes the time of year when the mystery of harmony within a disharmonious world appears to be most manifest. Wyn stands for the creation of harmony, comfort and the transformation of life for the better. Finally, the transformative runic half-month of Hagal also ends the Gregorian October, beginning its rulership on the *28th*.

Here, Hagal symbolises the underlying orderliness of all things, and also, in the north, denotes the beginning of the icy part of the year. According to Germanic tradition, the rune Hagal is called the Mother Rune, and this corresponds with the day of Fyribod, foreboding the icy winter-time.

In ancient times, the first day of October was the last day of the celebration of the Mysteries of Eleusis, called *Plemo Choai*, the earthen vessels. On a day sacred to the goddesses Demeter and Persephone, and their Roman parallels Ceres and Proserpina, this is the time of pouring out plenty.

In the *October 1st* ritual, two hallowed vessels were brought to the sacred place. One was set up towards the east, and the other to the west. Then they were overturned together, and the liquid they held fell to the earth as a libation. This rite of giving back to the earth reflects the ancient foundation ritual, where a cord is stretched between two pegs.

In the *Lux Madriana* calendar, the goddess month of Mala expires on *October 2nd*. It is followed by the month dedicated to the Egyptian goddess Hathor. This *Lux Madriana* month lies completely within the Gregorian October, ending on the *30th*.

Then, the final day of October, otherwise called hallowe'en or November Eve, is the first day of the month ruled by the goddess Samhain. This is the Irish name of the month of November.

OctobeR 4th

Ceres has another holy day, the Jejunium Cereris, which was one of the few fasts observed in Roman Paganism. It was instituted in the year 191 BCE as the result of consulting the oracle of the Sibylline Books.

In general, October is a month of goddesses of good fortune and luck. On the *7th*, the Nones of October, is the festival of the goddess Victoria, who is the personification of success and triumph, whilst on the *9th,* Felicitas, one of the Roman goddesses of good luck, is honoured along with Venus Victrix.

Then, on *October 12th* the Roman festival of Fortune Redux, the goddess of successful journeys and safe returns, whilst the following day is reserved for us to acknowledge the importance of holy wells, springs and fountains and their spiritual guardianesses.

In the Celtic tradition, we remember well-goddesses such as Coventina and Sirona and river-goddesses like Belisama, Dana, Sabrina and Sequana on this day.

The *13th* also marks the commencement of the runic half-month of Wyn, which is joy. In the contemporary Asatru, *October 14th* is celebrated as Winter's Day, which heralds the beginning of the winter part of the year, at which all summertime activities are terminated until Summer's Day comes after the long winter is ended in the following April.

Real Time in October is considerably different than local mean clock time, and therefore, in most places, even further from time-zone Mean Time. On *October 1st*, it is nearly ten minutes in front, and by the the *5th*, Real Time is running 11 and a half minutes earlier than clock time. As the month progresses, the sun continues to diverge from the clock.

On the *15th*, Real Time is running 13 minutes before clock time. The *19th* sees Real Time running 14 and a half minutes before clock time, and by the *26th*, it is a whole 16 minutes earlier than clock time. By Samhain eve, the last day of October, the clock and sun are almost 16 and a half minutes awry.

Novembeʀ

ovember is named as the ninth month of the Roman calendar. It is a powerful month of transformation through death, that commences with the most awesome festival in northern Paganism, Winter's Eve and Winter's Day, known to many Pagans as Samhain, the Irish festival of La Samhna.

In Celtic tradition, this is summer's end, which is also the end of the old year and the beginning of the new. So Winter's Eve and Winter's Day it is dedicated to goddesses of old endings and new beginnings. The Celtic reed-month of Ngetal occupies most of November, ending on the *24th*.

Novembeʀ 25th
The elder-tree month, Ruis commences. In Druidic tree-lore, the elder signifies that timeless oneness in which youth and age, life and death, are unified. The elder, at this time of year called Lady Elder, is the holy tree of to the Matron's or Mothers. Here, these three goddesses personify the triple female states of the human being as Girl, Mother and Old Woman.

At Samhain, Lady Elder is considered to embody particularly the third aspect of the Old Woman or Hag, in Celtic terms, the dangerous personage of The Cailleach, and in the Nordic tradition, the goddess Hela and the giantess Angrboda. The *Lux Madriana* calendar of the goddess has the month of Samhain present through almost all of the Gregorian November.

Here, the goddess is the personification of the time of year we celebrate now. The *Lux Madriana* Samhain month is followed on the *28th* by the month of Astraea. Followers of Asatr' call November Fogmoon, after the characteristic weather encountered at this time of year.

In the runic time-system of *The Way of the Eight Winds*, the Gregorian November begins during the half-month of Hagal. As this icy rune-influence ends, *November 13th* begins the runic half-month of Nyd.

This period is literally a time of need, when in traditional society every effort must be made to make preparations to survive the coming cold winter. Following the Nyd half-month, the period of the ice-rune Is commences on *November 28th*. Now is the deathly time when flow ceases, and we may be compelled to sit out bad weather in forced inertia.

The first of November is Winter's Day (Samhain or Calan gaeaf), one of the most powerful of the four fire festivals. Samhain is the third Station of the year, which is the time of awakening through death. Samhain is primarily the time of letting-go, when the plant dies and the seed falls to earth. At Samhain we abandon consciously with thanksgiving all of those things which once served us usefully but which now are superseded.

If we fail to give them away, we will have to continue to carry all of these unnecessary encumbrances in our everyday lives. But once we have abandoned them ceremonially, then we can leave them behind for ever, without looking back. That is the principle of letting-go.

Until Yuletide, this part of the year is a time of the fading light, when darkness is increasing, and the living world is apparently declining towards cessation. Samhain is thus the time of year when the link between the world of the living, and the Otherworld of the dead and non-human beings is at its most powerful.

Like all of the sacred days in the Northern Tradition, the observance of the Samhain festival begins at sunset on the previous eve.

This is Winter's Eve, the Welsh Nos Galan gaeaf, literally, the eve of the winter calends. Bonfire Night, one of the few collective folk-festivals still carried on all over Britain, is the transference of the Winter's Eve fire to a Protestant commemoration of a victory over Catholicism.

Although it is often called after the Catholic conspirer Guido Fawkes, who was hanged, drawn and quartered, Bonfire Night is focussed upon burning an effigy upon a fire which is the continuation of the pyramidal wooden structure called in the Irish tradition the *Torc tened* (fine boar) or *Torc calle* (boar of the forest), lit from the ashes of last year's fire.

In the Welsh tradition, this is one of the three *ysbryndnos* or spirit nights, the other two being May Eve and St John's Eve. On Nos Galan gaeaf, the spirits and wandering ghosts are walking the earth. Sometimes, they may be encountered in the form of *ladi* wen, the White Lady, whilst in other places, they may appear as the *hwch ddu gwta*, the Tail-less Black Sow, which appears to terrorise men.

Winter's Eve is the time when we recall the four sacred objects of the Otherworld that are manifestations of the European tradition of the four elements and their later appearance as the suits in the Tarot deck. These are the Stone of Destiny, the Spear of Lugh, the Cauldron of Regeneration and the invincible sword that manifests in all great swords like Excalibur and those made by the master swordsmiths, Ulfbehrt and Ingelrius.

They symbolise certain powers, recalled in the legend of the four Tuatha-da-Danaan women who are the supernatural bearers of these otherworldly treasures.

According to legend, they were visited one Samhain eve by the adventurer Red Hanrahan, who, sitting on a heather-grown bank in Sleive Echtge, noticed a door in the earth.

Entering a fine hall, he saw a high place at the opposite end, on which was enthroned a most beautiful woman. Below her, one step down, were four old, grey-headed Tuatha da Danaan women. Each of them held a different thing: one had a cauldron in her lap, another supported a huge stone on her knees; the third held a long-shafted spear, whilst the fourth grasped the hilt of an unsheathed sword.

Then the women arose, one by one. She with the cauldron said *"Pleasure"*. The second, the stone-carrier, called the word *"Power"*, whilst the third, brandishing the spear, declaimed the word *"Courage"*. The last woman, holding up the sword, said *"Knowledge"*. Then the women walked out, having given Hanrahan a valuable teaching on the meaning of the four symbolic artifacts of the Otherworld, both of their meaning and the function of women as guardianesses of the most sacred treasures of the earth.

These are acknowledged in the goddesses recalled in Nordic and Celtic myth as the guardianesses of the useful arts. Among them are Brigid, Fulla, Clidna, Gefn and Snotra.

The spiritual theme of the first part of November is of death and the relationship of the dead with the living. This takes the form of communion with the inhabitants of the Otherworld through ceremony, trance and divination. For On the side of the living, this is a time of personal purification when one gathers up that which one needs and looks towards the future.

In ancient Egyptian Paganism, the Isia, the festival of the goddess Isis, re-enacting the killing, ritual dismember-ment, reconstitution and resurrection of Osiris, was held from the first to the third of November. This theme of disintegration and reintegration perfectly encapsulates the nature of Samhain.

The Wild Hunt begins on Winter's Eve. This is the time of wintry storms, when the supernatural wild hunters ride through the sky, picking up those human beings who are unfortunate enough to get in the way. Often connected with Odin in his aspect as storm-god, the Wild Hunt is properly the preserve of Lady Percht or Frau Holle (Hela), the ruler of the underworld.

The spirit night of Winter's Eve is the epitome of her power, when ghosts, shades, sprites, spirits, demons and monsters are freed from the underworld to roam freely in this world for a little while. Perhaps now, but probably later, Frau Holle, in her active aspect as the White Lady, will cover the land with her white shroud of snow.

After sunset on *November 10th*, an observance of the Scottish goddess Nincnevin takes place. In contemporary understanding, Nincnevin is the northern goddess of hunting who rides with her entourage in a supernatural wild hunt through this night, taking away those who are unfortunate enough to be out in the night without magical protection.

During the French Revolution, the anticlerical revolutionists established a festival dedicated to the symbolic Goddess of Reason on this day. Although this was the first time she had been acknowledged under that name, goddesses of knowledge and understanding like Minerva, Saga and Snotra were venerated in older European Paganism.

In Paris, the festival of the goddess of Reason was celebrated in the dechristianized cathedral of Notre Dame, which the revolutionists converted into a Temple of Philosophy for the purpose. The veneration of the Goddess at Notre Dame was merely the recognition of the *anima loci* and the restoration of the elder faith at a Pagan sacred place. For the Parisian cathedral is the successor of earlier churches which superseded a great Pagan temple built on ground sacred to the Druids of Lutetia Parisiorum.

November 11th

Another festival of the dead, having been adopted in Britain as the day of remembrance of those slain in World War I, and subsequently every other war in which British forces have fought. This was a recognition of this time of year as a time of remembrance of the dead, transformed into a national day of mourning and pageantry.

November 11th is recognised in Ireland as the day of the blackthorn-sprites, the Lunantishees. These otherworldly beings who guard the sacred blackthorn, are most apparent on this day, standing in readiness to ward off any human being foolhardy enough to profane the holy thorns by cutting their wood now.

After sunset on *November 16th* is the time of Hecate Night, celebrated by some tendencies of wicca. Hecate Night celebrates her as the dark goddess of the underworld.

The otherworldly realm is manifested in this world through the musical harmonics and sacred geometry that are the physical expression of the Divine Harmony. Without this harmony, the cosmos would be chaos.

The goddess who is the earthly manifestation of these divine harmonious principles is revered on *November 22nd,* which is celebrated by all music-lovers as the day of St Cecilia.

Cecilia is the Christian version of the divine patroness of music, an aspect of the goddess Artemis Calliste, The Lily of Heaven. Cecilia was the spiritual guardianness of the medieval musicians' guilds and contemporary musicians acknowledge her as their spiritual muse.

John Dryden, in his A *Song for St Cecilia's Day* tells us:

"From harmony, from heavenly harmony,
This universal frame began;
From harmony to harmony
Thro' all the compass of the notes it ran,
The diapason closing full in man."

Continuing the November theme as month of the Otherworld, the *25th* is the day on which we acknowledge the goddesses of change and return. This goddess is known under many names, for she is the wheel-goddess of the underworld. So she is called variously Persephone, Proserpine, Kore, Arianrhod and Catherine. She is the Queen of the Shades, ruler of the spirits of the departed.

In an earlier period, *November 25th* was called Women's Merry-Making Day, upon which women's mysteries of life and death were celebrated. Five days later, the Gregorian month is brought to its close on the *30th* by the festival day of the country of Scotland, whose matronal goddess is the dangerous destroyer, Skadi *'The Scathing One'*.

Real Time at Samhain is running 16 and a half minutes ahead of the clock, the maximum divergence between the natural and artificial means of time-telling.

On *November 9th,* Real Time on this day is 16 minutes *'fast'* of the clock, and by the *16th* it is 15 minutes ahead of the clock. On the *23rd*, solar time stands 14 minutes fast of clock time. On the last day of the month, it is 11 and a half minutes in front of the local mean clock.

December

So-named after the tenth month of the Roman calendar, December contains the major festival celebrated by contemporary society, Christmas.

Like many of the festivals of this period, this is very patriarchal, exclusively celebrating the rebirth of the sun at midwinter, and playing down the origin of that birth. December is often seen as the time of preparation for the symbolic birth at midwinter of gods such as Osiris, Horus, Helios, Dionysus, Mithras and Jesus. Even in the Celtic tradition, the birth of the divine child, Pryderi, son of Rhiannon, is the main mythos of midwinter.

In Pagan Alexandria, however, the holy mother was acknowledged when the birth of the divine child was celebrated at the Koreion, the temple sacred to Kore. But, in general, unlike the rich goddess month of November, December has relatively few days dedicated to the female principle.

The midwinter solstice, called The Mother Night by contemporary Asatru followers, is the authentic Pagan Yule. In the Druidic observance of the Island of Britain, this is Alban Arthuan.

To contemporary Asatr', December is Wolfmoon. According to the runic time-cycles, the first part of December is under the regency of the ice-rune.

December 3rd

Is the festival of the Roman goddess Bona Dea, The Good Goddess. It is also the day of one of the three Germanic sister-goddesses, Einbet, Barbet and Wilbet, one of whose shrines was at the sacred place now occupied by Speyer Cathedral, burial place of many Holy Roman Emperors.

In medieval times, the goddess Barbet was assimilated with St Barbara. Although she is still revered in Catholic countries, St Barbara is no longer a saint, for her sanctity was abolished by the incumbent Pope of Rome in 1969, along with St George and St Christopher.

The then Pope of Rome decided that these, and other, sacred beings are 'no more than' mythological, and so he effectively excommunicated them from the Christian pantheon as unhistorical. Significantly, he hit the soft target of auxiliary saints, and did not decommission the equally mythic archangelic band under St Michael and the infernal hierarchy of Satan. Seemingly, literalism has infiltrated even the most symbolic of religious bodies, when key figures of a religion can be abolished simply because they are mythical.

Religious leaders who think like that should give up and join the atheists. As symbolic spiritual beings, however, Barbara and the others have not faded away into limbo, but have taken on an independent existence outside the official church.

Barbet has reassumed her position as a spiritual being in her own right, the goddess Barbara, who protects us and our buildings against being hit by lightning.

In Classical religion, the goddess Barbara is paralleled by Pallas Athene, who is the Roman goddess Minerva, the protectress-goddess of wisdom and patroness of the useful and elegant Arts. Her day is *December 4th*.

On *December 8th* in 1845, the astronomer Henke discovered the minor planet or asteroid that he named after the goddess Astraea. *December 10th* is the festival of *Lux Mundi*, the Light of the World, which, in goddess terms, celebrates the divinity of Liberty.

Allied to *Lux Mundi* is the day of St Lucy, the Lightbringer, which we celebrate on *December 13th*. Lucy is an aspect of the goddess Percht, as the lightbearer. Also known as Little Yule, this is a festival of lights in the darkness.

In Denmark, the eve of St Lucy's day is observed as a time for young women to practice divination to discover in advance the identity of their future husbands. The runic Jara period of Jara commences on St Lucy's Day.

Real Time on the first day of December is 11 and a half minutes fast of the clock. This is a time when solar time and clock time are rapidly coming together.

December 13th

Is superseded by the rune Jara, the rune of the year's completion. This straddles the winter solstice, and its stave-form resembles the Janus-figure associated with looking backwards and forwards at this turn of the solar year.

This rune, more than any other, encapsulates the cyclic nature of time and all life. Hopefully, if all is well, the Jara half-month should mark a period when events come to fruition after a year of correct action.

December 28th

Traditionally a bad day, Jara in turn is superseded by the runic half-month of Eoh This is the thirteenth rune, which in some of its aspects acts as the death rune. Here, it signifies the increasing coldness that comes as the days get longer.

The Celtic elder-tree month, Ruis continues until *December 22nd*. Then it is followed by no month, but an empty day, the intercalary day of *December 23rd*. This is a no-time that can last for more than one day, so that the winter solstice can come at the right time in relation to the new Celtic tree-cycle.

This elder-tree month is the end of the solar year, and the intercalary day is *"the secret of the unhewn stone"*. After the intercalary time comes the Celtic birch-month. This is named after the first character of the ogham alphabet, and is the sacred tree of the White Goddess as celebrated by Robert Graves. It signifies purification, manifested in the expulsion of all bad thoughts and influences, bringing new beginnings. According to the *Lux Madriana* calendar, the goddess month of Astraea ends on *December 25th*, being superseded on Boxing Day by the month of Hestia, which continues until Gregorian *January 22nd* in the new year.

The *7th* sees Real Time running 8 and a half minutes ahead of the clock, whilst by the *14th* it is only 5 and a half minutes ahead of the clock. On the *21st*, Real Time is only two minutes ahead of clock time, and on *December 25th*, the local mean clock and sun coincide, but as soon as the *28th*, Real Time is already running just over one minute slow of clock time.

Now the year is ended, and the goddesses have passed by in their cavalcade, bringing with them glimpses not only of otherworldly splendour, but also insights into our own states of being.

Appendix 1

The Lux Madriana Goddess Months

Hestia	December 26th - January 22nd
Bridhe	January 23rd - February 19th
Moura	February 20th - March 19th
Columbina	March 20th - April 17th
Maia	April 18th - May 15th
Hera	May 16th - June 12th
Rosea	June 13th - July 10th
Kerea	July 11th - August 8th
Hesperis	August 9th - September 5th
Mala	September 6th - October 2nd
Hathor	October 3rd - October 30th
Samhain	October 31st - November 27th
Astraea	November 28th - December 25th

Appendix 2

The Way of the Eight Winds Goddess Calendar

ccording to Northern Tradition observance, each of these days begins at sunset on the previous date, and ends at sunset. Thus, for instance, *May 1st*'s observance begins at sunset on *April 30th*, and ends at sunset on *May 1st,* the darkness following being the first part of *May 2nd*'s observance. Hence, the spirit-nights that precede the important festivals of the year.

January	(Month of Juno Antevorta and Juno Postvorta.)
1st	New Year. Lady Luck, Fortune, Arianrhod.
6th	Percht, the Weird Sisters
7th	Sekhmet
11th	The Nine Muses
30th	Goddesses of Peace

February   (Month of Juno Februa)

1st	Imbolc. Brigantia, Brigid
2nd	Iemanja
5th	Fortune, Tyche
14th	Sjofn
15th	Wolf-goddess
17th	Fornax, ovens

March   (Month of Hertha)

5th	The Ship of Isis
12th	Remembrance of the persecuted
15th	Rhea, Mother Earth, Fjorgynn
19th	Athena, Minerva
24th	Britannia
28th	Remembrance of our ancestors
30th	Concordia, harmony

April   (Month of Venus)

1st	Fortune Virilis, women's relationships with men
4th-11th	Cybele, the Great Mother
11th-19th	Ceres, the growing grain
23rd	Venus
28th	Flora, Blodeuwedd

May	(Month of Mía Majestas)
1st	Beltane.
3rd	Veneration of the Thorn, Monica
11th-13th	The Lemures, feeding the hungry ghosts
15th	Maia, Vesta, the sacred hearth
17th	Dea Dia
23rd	The Rosalia. Flora, Blodeuwedd
24th	The Mothers, the Three Mary's of the Sea
29th	Oak Apple Day. Ceres, Dia Dea

June	(Month of Juno, Queen of Heaven)
1st	Carna, Tempestas, Iansa
13th-15th	Minerva, Sulis, the Nine Muses, the Valkyries
24th	Spirit Night
27th	Aestas

July	(Month of Pax)
4th	Pax, goddess of peace
7th	Festival of Handmaidens
8th	Sol
10th	Holda, Heli and Skadi
15th	Rowana
21st	Salt Water
23rd	Fresh Water. Furrina
26th	Anna, Nanna, Nanan

August (Month of Demeter)

1st	Lammas. The Three Machas
12th	The Lights of Isis
13th	Hecate, Diana
15th	Diana, Our Lady
25th	Ops
27th	Isis
28th	Hathor

September (Month of Brigid)

8th	Our Lady
28th	Zisa

October (Month of Astraea)

4th	Jejeunius Cereris. Ceres
7th	Victoria
9th	Felicitas, Venus Victrix
12th	Fortune Redux
13th	Holy Wells and Sacred Rivers

November (Month of Hela)

1st	Samhain, Calan gaeaf
5th	Bonfire Night
10th	Nincnevin
11th	Lunantishees
16th	Hecate Night
22nd	Cecilia
25th	Persephone, Arianrhod, Catherine

December (Month of Rhiannon)

3rd	Bona Dea, Einbet Barbet, Wilbet, Barbara
10th	Lux Mundi
12th	Offerings to Isis
13th	Lucy, Percht
21st	Yule

Appendix 3

Sources of Further Information

In the British Isles, the following organisations assist, practice, teach and celebrate several areas of indigenous European spirituality. They are:

Dragon Environmental Group,
3, Sanford Walk,
London
SE14 6NB

The British Druid Order,
P. O. Box 29
St Leonards on Sea
East Sussex
TN37 7YP,

The Chapter of the Dragoness,
PO Box 3719,
London
SW17 8XT,

The Fellowship of Isis,
Foundation Centre,
Clonegal Castle,
Enniscorthy,
Republic of Ireland.

The Odinic Rite (I),
BCM Edda,
London
WC1N 3XX,

The Odinic Rite (II),
BCM Runic,
London
WC1N 3XX,

The Order of Bards, Ovates and Druids,
260 Kew Road,
Richmond,
Surrey
TW9 3EG,

The Pagan Federation,
BCM Box 7097,
London
WC1N 3XX,

The Way of the Eight Winds,
142 Pheasant Rise,
Bar Hill,
Cambridge
CB3 8SD,

Please include an SAE when writing to these organisations.

Appendix 4

The Stations of the Year

The structure of time is expressed in the East Anglian tradition through the Harvest Cycle. In this, the stages of the miracle of Bread are marked by eight stations, times of year that symbolise the progress of the cycle of life in terms of the plants life. Because the annual cycle is reflected by each day's round, each time of year, and hence each station correspondences, and the holy meanings of them.

Station	Festival	Time of Day	Event in the cycle
1	None	16.30	Death/rebirth-the parent plant brings forth the seed, then dies
2	Equinox	18.00	Calling-the ripening of the fruit and its harvesting

3	Samhain	21.00	Awakening-letting go, the seed falls to Earth
4	Yuletide	midnight	Enlightenment-rekindling of the light in the darkness
5	Equinox	06.00	Reconciliation-seemingly dead, the seed germinates
6	Beltane	09.00	Mystical Union-the growing plant is in full vigour, in harmony with the environment
7	Midsummer	noon	Sanctification-the flower opens and is fertilised
8	Lammas	15.00	Completion-the cycle begins anew

Bibliography

Deluciana: Von der Scheinenden Frau und der Wilden Percht - Von Barbarazweigen und Orakelnachten. Artemis, Stuttgart, 1995

Jones, Prudence: Sundial and Compass Rose: Eight-fold Time Division in Northern Europe. Fenris-wolf, Bar Hill, 1982.

Pennick, Nigel : A History of Pagan Europe, Routledge, London, 1995
Pennick, Nigel: The Pagan Source Book. Rider, London. 1992
Pennick, Nigel: Practical Magic in the Northern Tradition. Thoth, Loughborough, 1994
Pennick, Nigel: The Oracle of Geomancy. Capall Bann, Chieveley, 1995
Pennick, Nigel: Runic Astrology. Capall Bann, Chieveley, 1995
Pennick, Nigel: The Inner Mysteries of the Goths. Capall Bann, Chieveley, 1995
Pennick, Nigel: Secret Signs, Symbols and Sigils. Capall Bann, Chieveley, 1996

Index

FREE DETAILED CATALOGUE

A detailed illustrated catalogue is available on request, SAE or International Postal Coupon appreciated. Titles are available direct from Capall Bann, post free in the UK (cheque or PO with order) or from good bookshops and specialist outlets. Title currently available include:

Animals, Mind Body Spirit & Folklore
Angels and Goddesses - Celtic Christianity & Paganism by Michael Howard
Arthur - The Legend Unveiled by C Johnson & E Lung
Auguries and Omens - The Magical Lore of Birds by Yvonne Aburrow
Book of the Veil The by Peter Paddon
Call of the Horned Piper by Nigel Jackson
Cats' Company by Ann Walker
Celtic Lore & Druidic Ritual by Rhiannon Ryall
Compleat Vampyre - The Vampyre Shaman: Werewolves & Witchery by Nigel Jackson
Crystal Clear - A Guide to Quartz Crystal by Jennifer Dent
Earth Dance - A Year of Pagan Rituals by Jan Brodie

Earth Magic by Margaret McArthur
Enchanted Forest - The Magical Lore of Trees by Yvonne Aburrow
Healing Homes by Jennifer Dent
Herbcraft - Shamanic & Ritual Use of Herbs by Susan Lavender & Anna Franklin
In Search of Herne the Hunter by Eric Fitch
Inner Space Workbook - Developing Counselling & Magical Skills Through the Tarot
Kecks, Keddles & Kesh by Michael Bayley
Living Tarot by Ann Walker
Magical Incenses and Perfumes by Jan Brodie
Magical Lore of Animals by Yvonne Aburrow
Magical Lore of Cats by Marion Davies

Magical Lore of Herbs by Marion Davies
Masks of Misrule - The Horned God & His Cult in Europe by Nigel Jackson
Mysteries of the Runes by Michael Howard
Oracle of Geomancy by Nigel Pennick
Patchwork of Magic by Julia Day
Pathworking - A Practical Book of Guided Meditations by Pete Jennings
Pickingill Papers - The Origins of Gardnerian Wicca by Michael Howard
Psychic Animals by Dennis Bardens
Psychic Self Defence - Real Solutions by Jan Brodie
Runic Astrology by Nigel Pennick
Sacred Grove - The Mysteries of the Forest by Yvonne Aburrow
Sacred Geometry by Nigel Pennick
Sacred Lore of Horses The by Marion Davies
Sacred Ring - Pagan Origins British Folk Festivals & Customs by Michael Howard
Secret Places of the Goddess by Philip Heselton
Talking to the Earth by Gordon Maclellan
Taming the Wolf - Full Moon Meditations by Steve Hounsome
The Goddess Year by Nigel Pennick & Helen Field
West Country Wicca by Rhiannon Ryall
Witches of Oz The by Matthew & Julia Phillips

Capall Bann is owned and run by people actively involved in many of the areas in which we publish. Our list is expanding rapidly so do contact us for details on the latest releases. We guarantee our mailing list will never be released to other companies or organisations.

Capall Bann Publishing, Freshfields, Chieveley, Berks, RG20 8TF.